HV
9069
C38
1978

DATE DUE		
JAN 2 1 '0S	DEC 15 1995 S	
OCT 24 '0S		
DEC 1 6 '1S		
MAY 1 25		
JAN 29 '86'S		
OCT 8 88S		
JUL 2 8 1992		
DEC 0 6 1992		
NOV 2 0 1 25		
MAY 0 8 1996		

The Changing Faces of
Juvenile Justice

This book is published in conjunction
with the United Nations

**Monographs of the
United Nations Crime Prevention
and Criminal Justice Branch**

Dr. Kurt Neudek
General Editor

The Changing Faces of Juvenile Justice

Edited by
V. LORNE STEWART

New York • New York University Press • 1978

Permissions

I greatly appreciate the permission given by the following for use of passages from the works cited:

From "I, Too Nicodemis" by Curtis Bok Copyright 1946 by Alfred A. Knopf, Inc.

From "The Juvenile Court" by Barbara Wootton in the *Criminal Law Review* (October 1961), Sweet and Maxwell Ltd.

From "Protection of Children" by J.J. Kelso, an Ontario Government publication in 1911. Reprinted with permission of J.C. Thatcher, Queen's Printer for Ontario.

Library of Congress Cataloging in Publication Data

Main entry under title:

The Changing faces of juvenile justice.

(Monographs of the United Nations Crime Prevention and Criminal Justice Branch)
    Bibliography: p.
    Includes index.
    1. Juvenile justice, Administration of—Addresses essays, lectures.   2.   Juvenile corrections—Addresses essays, lectures.   I.   Stewart, V. Lorne.   II.   Series United Nations. Crime Prevention and Criminal Justice Branch. Monographs of the United Nations Crime Prevention and Criminal Justice Branch.
HV9069.C38   1978   364.6   77-87578
ISBN 0-8147-7788-0

In Memory of
JUDGE M. JAVIER DE YBARRA Y BERGE
President of the International Association of Youth Magistrates
1974-1977
who contributed greatly to the welfare of young people in Spain
and throughout the world.

Contents

Foreword
Gerhard O.W. Mueller

Chapter 1   Seeing Children Through Different Eyes   1
V. Lorne Stewart

Chapter 2   The Development of Juvenile Justice in   9
the United States
Orm W. Ketcham

Chaper 3   Prevention and Diversion in the United   43
States
Frederick Ward, Jr.

Chapter 4   Strategies for the Future of Juvenile   53
Corrections
Milton Luger

Chapter 5   As the Pendulum Swings in England and   69
Wales
Peter Marshall

ix

Chapter 6   The Scottish Rejection of the Juvenile   86
               Court
                   Beti Jones and G. J. Murray

Chapter 7   Juvenile Justice in Yugoslavia   111
                   Alenka Šelih

Chapter 8   The Swedish Approach to Juvenile   135
               Corrections
                   Ola Nyquist

Chapter 9   Tradition and Innovation in Child Care   151
               in Nigeria
                   Tolani Asuni

Chapter 10   The Faces of Juvenile Justice in Canada   157
                   V. Lorne Stewart

Foreword

If the world experience in juvenile justice could be summed up in one statement, it might come close to this: justice for the juvenile after the onset of delinquency is but a poor substitute for justice for the child in avoidance of delinquency. Justice for the child means a wholesome social environment in which the primary, the natural, organs of social control are still intact. A society which preserves its primary social control organs, needs few secondary social control organs. Where family, kinship, village, neighbourhood, and community are effective in the socialization of the young, and their integration into the communal stream, courts and prisons need not endeavor to do so when, for all practical purposes, it is too late to do so effectively, efficiently, and humanely. Yet, under the assault of urbanization, industrialization, mass communication, and heightened expectations, the traditional social control organs are crumbling—particularly fast in those parts of the world where crime prevention planning has not yet been incorporated in overall socioeconomic planning. That much is recognized everywhere. Divisions have occurred, however, on the responses to deal with the problem. Some countries are trying to shore up their traditional social control organs. Others are searching for surrogate social control organs to fit modern urbanized society. Still others have abandoned their hopes for social control and have swung over, almost entirely, to legal control. Among the latter one can find several directions, those subscribing to the doctrine of a benevolent *patria potestas* of the juvenile court and those who "adulterize" the postdelinquency juvenile justice system, either out of concern for the loss of procedural rights when benevolence takes the place of due process, or out of frustration when, seemingly, reformation does not work and retribution appears to be the only choice.

The world of juvenile justice is the world itself: the spectrum of experiences is global, the profile universal. If nations have not learned from each other, then it is only because they did not understand each other and each other's experiences. Since its inception the United Nations has endeavored to make this global laboratory universally accessible. Many governmental and nongovernmental organizations, among them especially the International Association of Youth Magistrates (IAYM), have been of invaluable assistance in this regard. It goes to the credit of Judge V. Lorne Stewart, a vice-president of IAYM, that the theme was dealt with at a special seminar conducted in conjunction with the Fifth United Nations Congress on the Prevention of Crime and the Treatment of Offenders, and that it was accepted by the Committee on Crime Prevention and Control as one of the five topics of the Sixth United Nations Congress on the Prevention of Crime and the Treatment of Offenders. "Juvenile Justice—Before and After the Onset of Delinquency" will now command global attention, in the recognition that few if any social problems in the world today are as significant for the ultimate survival of humankind. To help us all focus on the topic, Judge Stewart has assembled the experiences and views of some of the most outstanding and representative workers in the field, from a broad spectrum of cultures. The experience is now before us. We have but to choose our path.

Gerhard O.W. Mueller
Professor of Law and Criminal Justice
Chief, United Nations Crime Prevention and
Criminal Justice Branch

Acknowledgments

A special appreciation is extended to Mrs. Clare Spurgin O.B.E., J.P. (first woman president of the International Association of Youth Magistrates, 1966–70) for her sincere and generous support of this project and for her worldwide service on behalf of youth.

Several "lions of criminology" have, through their interest, encouragement, and advice, stimulated the production of this book. Most of the authors have felt the personal influence of these scholars. Our appreciation is both composite and individual in nature. The late Dr. Hermann Mannheim, Sir Leon Radzinowicz, Professor Sheldon Glueck and the late Dr. Eleanor Glueck, Professor Monrad Paulsen, Dr. Thorsten Sellin, and Dr. Marvin E. Wolfgang have all been active behind the scenes in one way or another, and the book would not have been written without them. Professor Alvar Nelson of Uppsala Universited and Dr. S.K. Mukherjee of the Australian Institute of Criminology assisted by providing background information.

The Laidlaw Foundation of Toronto, the Russell Sage Foundation of New York, and the Solicitor General of Canada have all assisted financially at various points in time, a fact greatly appreciated. They are, however, in no way responsible for the contents of this book.

Graduate students at the University of Toronto in the Centre of Criminology have assisted in the preliminary study of juvenile justice systems for a number of years. Their correspondence with students, professors, and government officals and others in a number of countries has brought together a library of national statutes, articles, and reports now available to interested scholars.

Thanks is due Diane Finkel, Carole Ghazal, Carole McMahon, and Veronica Corbett for their assistance with respect to many details including the preparation of this manuscript.

V. Lorne Stewart

Contributors

TOLANI ASUNI, President of the African Psychiatric Society; Department of Psychiatry Ahmadu-Bello University, Lagos, Nigeria. A member of the United Nations Committee on Crime Prevention and Control. A pioneer and authority on the treatment of offenders.

BETI JONES, Chief Social Work Adviser, Social Work Services Group, Scottish Office, Edinburgh, Scotland. Responsible for the evolution of the Social Work (Scotland) Act, 1968 and the institution of the panel system for the treatment of children in need or who are offending. Graduate of the University of Wales and Honorary Fellow in the Department of Social Administration.

ORM W. KETCHAM, Juvenile Justice Project Director of the National Center for State Courts, Williamsburg, Virginia; former Judge of the Juvenile Court of the District of Columbia; former Associate Judge, the Superior Court of the District of Columbia; Adjunct Professor of Law, University of Virginia Law School. B.A. (Princeton), Ll.B. (Yale). Coauthor of *Juvenile Justice and Cases and Materials Relating to Juvenile Courts* by Ketcham and Paulsen; Executive Vice-President of the International Association of Youth Magistrates (1966-74).

MILTON LUGER, V.P., Odyssey Institute, Sydney, Australia, Former Assistant Administrator of the Office of Juvenile Justice and Delinquency Prevention in the Law Enforcement

Assistance Administration in Washington, D.C. Formerly Director of the Division for Youth of New York State. Has written widely on delinquency topics. Attended Columbia University.

PETER MARSHALL, Deputy Assistant Commissioner and Director of Information, New Scotland Yard, London.

G. J. MURRAY, Central government administrator, Scottish office, Edinburgh, Scotland. Involved in the setting up and operation of the children's panel system.

OLA NYQUIST, Member of the Swedish Parliament; Chairman of the Regional University Organization of Uppsala. Received Ll.B., Ll.M., and Ll.D. degrees at the University of Uppsala. Postgraduate studies at Cambridge. Has taught at the University of Uppsala. Author of *Juvenile Justice,* a comparison of the Swedish Child Welfare Boards and the California Juvenile Courts, including the California Youth Authority.

ALENKA ŠELIH, Professor of Criminology at the Institute of Criminology, University of Lujbljani, Yugoslavia. Has written widely in the area of juvenile delinquency and child welfare.

V. LORNE STEWART, Expert Consultant on Juvenile Justice, United Nations Crime Prevention and Criminal Justice Branch in New York; Former senior judge of the Provincial Court (Family Division) for the Judicial District of York (Toronto); Consultant to the Canada Law Reform Commission on juvenile matters; member of the Solicitor General of Canada's Legislation Committee on Juvenile Justice; Permanent Fellow of the Centre of Criminology, University of Toronto. Has taught at the University of Toronto. Attended the Universities of Saskatchewan, Toronto, and Pennsylvania. Author of: *The Development of Juvenile Justice in Canada, Courts and Boards Exercising Jurisdiction over Children,* and *Three and a Half Steps Toward Juvenile Justice in Canada.* Coauthor of: *Age and Responsibility,* and *The*

Pre-Judicial Exercise of Discretion and Its Impact on Children. Coeditor of: *Youth Crime and Juvenile Justice: International Perspectives.*

Vice-President and representative of the International Youth Magistrates Association on the Alliance of Non-Governmental Organizations at the United Nations. Vice-President of the Alliance.

FREDERICK WARD, JR., Executive Vice-President of the National Council on Crime and Delinquency, Hackensack, New Jersey. Responsible for the Information Center and Library, Research Center, Training Center, Legal Department, Youth Development Center, staff specialists in law enforcement, courts, correction and demonstration projects. Has served as adviser and consultant to government on aspects of criminal justice. Has attended the University of London and the New York School of Social Work at Columbia University.

1

Seeing Children Through Different Eyes

V. Lorne Stewart

The pendulum of juvenile justice has swung in wide arcs in many places during recent years. There is every indication that it will continue its nervous and restless response to changes in social and political philosophy, to public alarm over acts of violence by young people, and to the accelerated application of the skills of educators, behavioral and social scientists, and sociologists to the problems that surround youth. The juvenile court is but one actor in this drama that starts early in the life of a child—perhaps much earlier than we had anticipated—with the plot unfolding in a gradual, relatively uneventful fashion with many youngsters but in a much more explosive and rebellious manner with others. But appearances may be deceiving. The quiet, unresponding youngster lost or hidden in the womb of the home or classroom may be engaged in an inner warfare of distressing proportions. Who can tell where his fear, indecision, and rebellion may take him? When, within the broad expanse of child development, we separate out, perhaps ghettoize, and designate a part of the whole as the property of juvenile justice, is there not a danger that we may be capturing those that should be treated otherwise? Where do we draw the line between the child who needs care and protection and the one who needs to be controlled by extraneous inventions such as the juvenile court? If the community agencies cannot control the uncontrollable,

1

who can? If it falls the lot of the juvenile court to do by authority what schools, agencies, and clinics cannot do by persuasion, what kind of court must it be? How much more than law must the judge know if he or she is to be the leader of a team of corrective experts too frequently dealing with the child "from the other side of the tracks"? Must a type of professional esperanto be invented so they can understand and accept one another? Or is the pendulum swinging in some other direction?

In this volume an attempt has been made to bring to the reader the thinking of a number of persons with long experience in relevant areas, including the judiciary, psychiatry, social work, corrections administration, education, police, and politics. The viewpoints expressed are those of the individual authors and may or may not be representative. However, it could prove useful to listen to people whose opinions have been formed on the firing line of juvenile justice and who have weathered many changes in policy and practice in the pursuit of the best way to deal with delinquent children. This volume, then, consists of case profiles of the juvenile justice systems in a number of countries drawn by persons actively involved in the process.

After many years as a juvenile and family court judge, the opportunity presented itself in 1965 to launch out on an adventure that took me to many places around the world and into the company of men and women of rare ability, knowledge, and skill in the art and science of dealing with young people. Some were scholars who had devoted years to teaching and research. Others were judges faced with similar human problems but who had inherited different systems of justice. There were administrators, probation officers, policemen, social workers, clinicians, and many young people themselves. However, the greatest impetus came from a Saturday morning's discussion in 1965 with Professor Monrad Paulsen in his office at Columbia University concerning the pending case of Gerald Gault and the future of juvenile justice.

2

Through the support of the Laidlaw and Russell Sage Foundations, it was possible to meet people in Denmark, the Federal Republic of Germany, the German Democratic Republic, Poland, the USSR, France, Italy, Spain, Switzerland, England, Scotland, the United States, Jamaica, the Cayman Islands and Canada. It was obvious that each country had its own way of looking at its problem young people. This was to be expected. Even within countries there were parochial and individual differences. However, there was an eagerness on the part of those close to the problem to know what was happening elsewhere. Searching for better ways to deal with their own children, they wanted to hear about successful efforts in other countries. This seemed to me to be a laudable attitude and one worthy of support and cooperation. In 1971 I formulated a proposal entitled "A Multi-National Study of Juvenile Justice Systems and Alternatives" with the object in mind of engaging in a cross-national survey of the attitudes, the practices, and the effectiveness of such systems. While it did not prove possible to follow through with the study at that time, the proposal was sent to the United Nations Social Defense Research Institute in Rome in 1971 stressing the urgency for such research and the sharing of experience. The faces of juvenile justice were changing around the world and people, perplexed by the problems of youth, were desperately searching for new answers to old problems.

In 1975 an invitation was received to organize a seminar on "Juvenile Corrections" as part of the ancillary program of the Fifth United Nations Congress on the Prevention of Crime and the Treatment of Offenders to be held in Toronto. Some twenty persons agreed to prepare papers on various aspects of the subject. Due to unforeseen circumstances, the venue of the congress was transferred to Geneva. This created a serious problem for some of the participants. Fortunately, it was possible for seven of them to take part in the Geneva program. The title of the seminar was changed to "Juvenile Justice in Profile." Papers were rewritten to focus upon this subject giving an outline of the preventive services available; describing the justice procedures from the point of police contact on through the "day in court"; and discussing the use of postcourt correctional services in each country.

The Geneva seminar was supported by the Alliance of Non-Governmental Organizations on Crime Prevention and Criminal Justice and by the International Association of Youth Magistrates. The response of those attending the meetings was spirited and resulted in the presentation of a petition to the United Nations asking that the topic of juvenile justice be given an official place on the agenda of the next congress to be held in Australia in 1980.

The panel presentations and discussion in Geneva largely form the basis of the chapters in this book. Papers written for Toronto, but not used in Geneva, along with others being prepared by persons in several other countries, will form the body of a second volume on juvenile justice.

Orm W. Ketcham acted as vice-chairman of the seminar. His judicial experience, so highly recognized in the United States, extends well beyond the boundaries of that country. For many years he has been a member of the International Association of Youth Magistrates, serving as one of its consultants. He agreed to write his chapter of this book in such a way that, along with those by Frederick Ward and Milton Luger, the juvenile justice system in the United States would be fully described and analyzed. His viewpoint embraces the thought that there is more than one road through the laws and procedures of juvenile justice and child development. Whether by means of the high road of the court or the low road of administrative boards and panels, the hoped-for destination is the same. Who gets there first, or at all, only time, experience and intelligent research will tell. In the meantime, the important thing is that while recognizing that time is still on our side when dealing with children, the country is wise that does not hold to the status quo in this matter but moves on through amendment, innovation, and action to make society a safe and adventuresome place for children and the young person responsible in his or her freedom.

Frederick Ward deals with the swing of the pendulum toward community-based services in the United States. He sees in this a general social reform movement that may result in the reduction of alienation among the young, the poor, and members of minority groups. The change is not without conflict, however, as counterbalancing pressures push in two directions at the same time. There are those who wish to attack the problem without court intervention but others who want to see some juveniles, as young as fourteen years, dealt with in adult criminal courts and institutions. Reference is made to the efforts of the National Council on Crime and Delinquency to remove status offenses from the jurisdiction of the courts and to its definitive study of Youth Service Bureaus done by the late Sherwood Norman.

Milton Luger, former Assistant Administrator of the Office of Juvenile Justice and Delinquency Prevention of the Law Enforcement Administration in Washington, and now with the McGrath Foundation in Sydney, Australia, discusses strategies for the future of corrections. He sees no magic in incarceration but from many years of experience as head of the New York State Division of Youth recognizes the size and complexity of the problem facing the courts. He rightly stresses the need for communities to shore up their defenses and for agencies to improve their services while at the same time attempting through innovation to meet the new challenges presented by youth.

Peter Marshall, Deputy Assistant Commissioner and Director of Information of New Scotland Yard brings to the book the concerns of the police and of magistrates in England and Wales about the rise in youth crime and the inability of the "Children and Young Persons' Act" to cope with it. Trained in the law and with many years of experience in London, his chapter is a perceptive and frightening analysis of what can happen when the pendulum begins to swing too far, too fast.

5

The Scottish chapter by Beti Jones and George Murray shows how far the pendulum can swing from traditional juvenile justice and still hold public support and function effectively. Scotland has abolished the juvenile court and has established a panel system consisting of lay participants. Unlike the lay magistracy of England, these persons are nonjudicial and function within a different framework. This chapter tells how this is done. The sound judgment of Jones and Murray has been confirmed in an empirical study by Bruce and Spencer.[1] However, there are those who have raised serious questions about the system.[2]

Professor Šelih describes how delinquents are treated in Yugoslavia. She stresses the importance of adequate social and educational services for children under fourteen years of age. This is a timely chapter written by a careful and sensitive scholar and practitioner at a time when the school is being seen with renewed clarity as a bulwark against crime.

The Swedish experience is carefully analyzed by Dr. Nyquist, who has long been an author and expert in these matters. His chapter undoubtedly will raise some serious questions. The reader will be interested to see how one country (along with all of the other Scandinavian countries) has been able to deal with recalcitrant young people without a juvenile court.

The importance of the family, tribe, and community emphasized in Dr. Asuni's chapter is of great significance. As other

----

1. Bruce, N. and Spencer, Prof. J.: "Face to Face With Families" Edinburgh. Macdonald Publishers, 1976.
2. Curran, J.H.: "The Children's Hearing System: A Review of Research".
    Scottish Office
    Central Research Unit
    Edinburgh.
    Her Majesty's Stationery Office 1977.

countries take stock of their procedures, this provocative thesis from a leading psychiatrist in the Third World cannot be ignored. While the chapter, unfortunately, is short it does cut through to fundamental issues.

The eagerness with which the subject of juvenile justice is being examined in various parts of the world may be the result in part of the turbulence created by the Gerald Gault storm in the United States. However, it would appear that much more is involved. People in many places are beginning to see children through different eyes. Furthermore, there is a growing conviction that if we want to prevent crime, we will have to start earlier in the process. This obviously binds us all together in one bundle, including the professions, and commits each to provide knowledge about human behavior and the means to control it so that "after all the blaming stops" we can start to cooperate toward the discovery of more positive solutions and to give more ample support to agencies that are functioning successfully. Legislation without the means to implement it is an exercise in futility.

The chapters in this volume are in a sense a microcosm of thought about children in trouble written by persons actively involved in crime prevention and criminal justice in various parts of the world.

2

The Development of Juvenile Justice
in the United States

Orm W. Ketcham

Four or five decades ago brash American sociologists proudly described the juvenile court as one of their greatest inventions.[1] Almost in the same breath American jurists asserted that the juvenile court was a legal descendant of the English chancery concept of *parens patriae*.[2] Today critical scholars are suggesting less altruistic reasons for the self-righteous emotionalism that spawned the first juvenile court act in Illinois in 1899.[3] The truth probably lies somewhere between.

Until the industrial revolution at the beginning of the nineteenth century, a child was of value chiefly to his parents or family. In that agrarian society children were called upon—even forced—to do chores and drudgery at an early age, but only in the home or on the farm. The rapidly growing factories, mines, and shops of the Victorian era had a sudden need for docile,

---

1. Van Waters, "Organization of Family Court," *The Child, the Clinic and the Court,* New Republic (1925).
2. Lindsay v. Lindsay, 257 Ill. 328, 100 N. E. 892 (1913).
3. Platt, *The Child Savers—The Intervention of Delinquency,* U. of Chicago Press (1969); Fox, *Juvenile Justice Reform: An Historical Perspective,* 22 Stan. L. Rev. 1187 (1970).

strong, and supple young workers. Thus, children became an exploited economic force—a minority class which elicited great sympathy from social reformers in the second half of the nineteenth century. As a result, in 1899 a group of affluent women reformers in the state of Illinois in the heartland of developing America joined prominent lawyers and social workers to push through a statute which established the first independent juvenile court.

The popularity and emotional appeal of this tangible concern for other people's oppressed, downtrodden, and morally debauched children was all-conquering. Most American states quickly followed Illinois's lead and passed statutes which created juvenile court jurisdictions. Many such statutes oozed selfrighteousness and admonished kindly judges, like good fathers, to lead misguided youths to salvation by any means that was available. By the time the New York Stock Exchange crashed in 1929 signaling the Great Depression, all but two states in the United States had some version of a juvenile court act.[4] Although in many states this new court was administered by the same judge and personnel as the criminal court and sat only one day a week as a juvenile court, the philosophical principle had swept the nation.

Several questions are raised by these events in the United States.

1. What social and legal circumstances evoked the juvenile justice system?
2. Did the advent of the juvenile court herald new independence for children and youth, or was it merely an expression of noblesse oblige by a parent-dominated society?

---

4. Tappan, *Juvenile Delinquency,* 172-173, McGraw-Hill (1949).

3. Is the juvenile court a new legal process or merely a device for enforcing social work?
4. Will the juvenile justice system help strengthen the American family structure, or will it replace and thus erode the family?
5. Will the juvenile justice system be durable and carve out a permanent place in the judicial structure, or will it be "swept away by the tide of legal history"?[5]
6. How does the juvenile justice system coordinate or interact with judicial procedures for adjudicating and correcting adult criminals?

The American origins of the juvenile court movement as a means of breaking away from the rigidities and retributive principle of criminal law were set forth in some detail in Lou, *Juvenile Courts in the United States*:

> The juvenile court is conspicuously a response to the modern spirit of social justice. It is perhaps the first legal tribunal where law and science, especially the science of medicine and those sciences which deal with human behavior, such as biology, sociology, and psychology, work side by side. It recognizes the fact that the law unaided is incompetent to decide what is adequate treatment of delinquency and crime. It undertakes to define and readjust social situations without the sentiment of prejudice. Its approach to the problem which the child presents is scientific, objective, and dispassionate. The methods which it uses are those of social casework, in which every child is studied and treated as an individual.

---

5. Ketchum, "The Unfulfilled Promise of the Juvenile Court," *Justice for the Child* 38, Free Press of Glencoe (1962).

These principles upon which the juvenile court acts are radically different from those of the criminal courts. In place of judicial tribunals, restrained by antiquated procedure, saturated in an atmosphere of hostility, trying cases for determining guilt and inflicting punishment according to inflexible rules of law, we have now juvenile courts, in which the relations of the child to his parents or other adults and to the state or society are defined, and are adjusted summarily according to the scientific findings about the child and his environments.[6]

Others who wrote about these events were often more eloquent and more emotional.[7] There were, in addition, authors who set about reconciling the juvenile court process with the criminal justice system through its alleged origins in the English common law and equity courts.

The conception that the State owes a duty of protection to children that it does not owe to adults was established by the old courts of equity. From the earliest times children have been regarded as the wards of chancery. The crown was parens patriae and exercised its prerogative to aid unfortunate minors through the great seal.[8]

In past generations American criminal courts had asked but one question: "Has he or she committed a crime?" As Judge Julian Mack, one of the articulate legal spokesmen for the new juvenile court movement, said:

6. U. of No. Car. Press (1927) at p. 2.
7 Lathrop, "Introduction" to Breckinridge, *The Delinquent Child and the Home,* Charities Pub. Comm. N.Y. (1912).
8. Flexner & Oppenheimer, *The Legal Aspect of the Juvenile Court,* 9 Children's Bureau Pub. No. 99 (1922).

Today, however, the thinking public is putting another sort of question. Why is it not just and proper to treat these juvenile offenders, as we deal with the neglected children, as a wise and merciful father handles his own child whose errors are not discovered by the authorities? Why is it not the duty of the state, instead of asking merely whether a boy or a girl has committed a specific offense, to find out what he is, physically, mentally, morally, and then if it learns that he is treading the path that leads to criminality to take him in charge, not so much to punish, as to reform, not to degrade but to uplift, not to crush but to develop, not to make him a criminal but a worthy citizen.[9]

In some instances, challenges to the constitutionality of the new, exceedingly discretionary juvenile court acts caused appellate courts to review their legal antecedents. In briefs before state appellate courts, where reverence for the past as precedent was especially powerful, legal researchers put forth the claim that these new laws were, in reality, only an extension of the doctrine enunciated in a few decisions of English chancery courts— the principle of *parens patriae*. When the chancery court was obliged to interfere in the feudal or moral affairs of young, titled heirs to property, it insisted that these were but juvenile subjects of the ruler. Hence, the king as *parens patriae* could lawfully exercise jurisdiction over the children or their property. Those seeking approval of the juvenile court statutes insisted that America had inherited this concept along with English common law.

Although the analogy between an English feudal king and an elected judge in a democratically organized American state was a bit strained, it was enthusiastically adopted by most appellate courts. With a hoot and a holler the juvenile court, with its in-

---

9. Mack, *The Juvenile Court,* 23 Harvard L. Rev. 104 (1909).

stant legal heritage, was swiftly and generally approved by the legal profession. Glowing reports and articles of justification heralded the new mode for saving juveniles from criminality.[10]

But the model for the juvenile justice system was the social science or medical model—something with which the legal profession was not familiar. So, almost as quickly and effortlessly as it was found to be constitutional, the juvenile court was forgotten by lawyers and judges. Most juvenile courts in the 1930s and 1940s became the province of social workers and often were listed in the telephone directory in columns reserved for social agencies. With the flight of lawyers from the scene, early efforts by men like Judge Julian Mack to surround juvenile court procedure with concepts of legal due process were discarded. Social workers and juvenile court personnel soon found it easier to cloak their actions—like the feudal kings from whom they allegedly inherited their authority—with the adage that the "king can do no wrong." It was stated that a juvenile court judge was not judging or punishing children brought before the court but acting in their best interest in order to save them from criminal careers and moral degradation. If that were so, there was no justification for the adversary system nor for lawyers to challenge the court's authority by appellate review of its dispositions. According to this reasoning, the treated or saved child had no need for protection from the court.

Thus, in the United States between World War I and the end of World War II, a system for handling delinquent, errant, and neglected children developed essentially outside the American legal structure. The slogans of the juvenile justice system in those days were not due process of law but salvation, protective custody, and unerring faith in the efficacy of social science. One well-known, redemptive juvenile institution proclaimed: "There

---

10. Lou, *Juvenile Courts in the United States,* U. of No. Car. Press (1927) p. 2.

14

is no such thing as a bad boy.'' Social workers devotedly sought new methods to lead misguided youth back to paths of productive righteousness. Since there appeared to be no disagreement about what was "right," there was hardly a need for trials or contested hearings. In fact, some juvenile judges even contended that the new juvenile justice system heralded a nobler and more scientific process untrammeled by law or legalisms.[11]

After World War II, disillusionment with the new order emerged. Significant numbers of young persons, even after being counseled and guided by fatherly juvenile judges and qualified social workers, failed to be "saved" and continued in their antisocial behavior. Apologists insisted that these failures only pointed to insufficient appropriations and facilities. But the misbehavior of many of these unrepentant youths was alarmingly similar to the criminal acts of adult offenders. A restless citizenry became concerned about the growing lawlessness, mobility, and violence that ushered in the 1950s. And lawyers—both prosecutors and defense attorneys—were uneasy with the lack of due process in juvenile courts and the unrestrained discretion of juvenile court judges.

This unrest was articulated in the law journals and in the writings of legal scholars in and out of the law schools. Whether these articles encouraged lawyers to return to the juvenile courts they had created half a century earlier and then deserted, or whether the gradual return of lawyers to these children's courts sparked the growth of critical articles is a "chicken-or-egg" question. Suffice it to say that the interaction kicked up a legal storm in the late 1950s and the 1960s, a period noted for its concern for equality and legal rights. A sampling of the titles from that era reveals the thrust of their challenge: "The Rights of Juvenile Delinquents, An Appraisal of Juvenile Court Pro-

---

11. Schramm, "The Judge Meets the Boy and His Family," in *National Prob. Assoc. Yearbook* (1945) pp. 182-194.

cedures,"[12] "Fairness to Juvenile Offenders,"[13] "The Juvenile Court—Benevolence in the Star Chamber,"[14] "Juvenile Court—A Labyrinth of Confusion for the Lawyer,"[15] "How Far Can Court Procedure Be Socialized Without Impairing Individual Rights?,"[16] "The Juvenile Court and the Limits of Juvenile Justice,"[17] "The Juvenile Court: Effective Justice or Benevolent Despotism?"[18]

Legal challenges followed and appellate courts were called upon to analyze and appraise the operation of the juvenile court process—or lack of it. In the first half century of the juvenile court movement in the United States there had been amazingly few analytical judicial rulings on the process. Only the philosophy of the system had been considered in the formative years. After the early rush to acclaim the new order and give it constitutional legitimacy appellate challenges ceased. Never had the Supreme Court of the United States interpreted a juvenile court act.[19] Thus, the stage was set for sweeping new mandates, and legal scholars begged for judicial decision and guidance.

In the District of Columbia a progressive and active U.S. Court of Appeals produced several significant rulings pioneering in the juvenile due process field. As early as 1956 the case of *Shioutakon* v. *District of Columbia* established the right of

---

12. Lewis, 47 J. Crim. L., C. & P.S. No. 5 (1957).
13. Paulsen, 58 Minn. L. Rev. 547 (1960).
14. Beemsterboer, 50 J. Crim. L., C. & P.S. No. 5 (1960).
15. Molloy, 4 Ariz. L. Rev. 1 (1962).
16. Waite, 52 J. Crim. L., C. & P.S. No. 12 (1962).
17. Allen, 11 Wayne L. Rev. 676 (1965).
18. Polow, 53 A.B.A.J. 31 (1967).
19. Cases such as Haley v. Ohio, 322 U.S. 596 (1948) and Gallegos v. State of Colorado, 370 U.S. 49 (1962) had only dealt with the application of criminal law principles to defendants under eighteen years of age.

counsel for juveniles in the federal capital.[20] Thus, it was not surprising that the first case in which the Supreme Court interpreted a juvenile court statute came from the District of Columbia's Juvenile Court in 1966. *Morris Kent* v. *United States* was only tangentially concerned with juvenile court procedures; it involved a sixteen-year-old youth charged with several armed robberies and several rapes who was transferred from the juvenile to the adult federal court and was tried and convicted by adult criminal standards of due process. But the Supreme Court took the opportunity of its remand of this case for more formal transfer procedures to comment broadly about the unrestrained discretion exercised by juvenile court judges. Thus, the *Kent* opinion was a harbinger of major decisions to follow.

The seminal decision came the next year. Like the Great Divide, *In the Matter of Gerald Gault*[21] constitutes the watershed for legal issues in the juvenile justice system. Scholars, law professors, and law students regularly identify procedures and cases as pre-Gault or post-Gault. The Supreme Court, speaking through Justice Abe Fortas, ordered that in every state or federal case in which a juvenile is charged with a criminal offense for which he or she can be incarcerated the juvenile court must provide: (1) timely written notice of the specific charges; (2) the right to appointed legal counsel; (3) the right to confront sworn witnesses and cross-examine them; and (4) the constitutional privilege against self-incrimination.

The Supreme Court's decree that juveniles must be given these four major elements of due process of law pushed the juvenile justice system into the thick of national constitutional issues. At

---

20. 98 U.S. App. D.C. 371, 236 F. 2d 666 (1956); See also In Re Custody of a Minor, 108 U.S. App. D.C. 18, 250 F. 2d 419 (1957) and Harling v. United States, 111 U.S. App. D.C. 174, 295 F. 2d 161 (1961).
21. 387 U.S. 1, 87 S. Ct. 1428, 18 L. Ed. 2d 527 (1967).

first, there were expressions of concern from many quarters.[22] Determined efforts were made to limit the legal impact of *Gault* by narrow interpretations or by modifications in juvenile justice operations. And many juvenile court judges either gave its mandates lip service or ignored them altogether and continued to act "in the best interest of the child," as he or she interpreted that phrase with unbridled discretion from day to day.

But the demands for more equal and predictable justice in juvenile courts were not to be denied. By extraordinary coincidence, a Presidential Commission on Law Enforcement and Administration of Justice had issued its Report[23] calling for a major overhaul of the juvenile justice system only four months before the *Gault* decision. The *Gault* decision and the President's Commission Report unleashed a pent-up flood of legal appeals as well as reappraisals of philosophy.[24] Nearly every state's appellate court was called upon to follow the broad and revolutionary requirements of *Gault* in numerous challenges to varied state statutes. Many state supreme courts quickly followed the Supreme Court's guidelines and vastly modified local practices. Some resisted and national appeals followed. In the next three years the Supreme Court ruled that a juvenile's guilt must be established beyond a reasonable doubt,[25] thus adding

22. National Council of Juvenile Court Judges, Resolution adopted at 30th Annual Conference, Fort Lauderdale, Florida (1967); Polier, *The Gault Case: Its Practical Impact on the Philosphy and Objectives of the Juvenile Court,* 1 Fam. L. Q. 47 (1967).

23. *The Challenge of Crime in a Free Society,* U.S. Government Printing Off. (1967) pp. 55-89.

24. George, *Gault and the Juvenile Court Revolution,* P.L.I. (1967) pp. 79-117.

25. In re Winship, 397 U.S. 358, 90 S. Ct. 1068, 25 L. Ed. 2d 368 (1970).

another major element of due process to the legal rights afforded a juvenile. Although the Supreme Court had not specifically declared that a juvenile had a right of appeal (and hence the right to a transcript of judicial proceedings) in its *Gault* opinion, no one really doubted that this right existed. It has been honored in most if not all jurisdictions.

The flood tide of legal change, loosed by *Gault*, swept through all of the fifty American states as well as the District of Columbia and other jurisdictional enclaves. Explicit and detailed decisions on a wide variety of legal issues relating to the juvenile justice system poured forth like mountain floods coursing down a dry streambed. By conservative estimate there have been ten times as many appellate decisions in American juvenile cases in the nine post-*Gault* years than were written in all the sixty-eight years pre-*Gault*. Thus, at the state level, most of this revolution occurred on a case-by-case basis as appeal courts followed *Gault* and its progeny. But a good deal of change also occurred through statutory revisions and the overhaul of juvenile codes in nearly half of the states. Uniform Acts were developed[26] and the U.S. Department of Health, Education, and Welfare even published a *Legislative Guide for Drafting Family and Juvenile Court Acts*.[27]

Some hoped that all of the constitutional rights assured to adult criminal defendants by the U.S. Constitution (and required to be provided by the states by the Fourteenth Amendment to the U.S. Constitution) would soon be made available to juvenile respondents. But the tide turned, and the Supreme Court refused to go all the way. In a majority opinion written by Justice Blackmun in *McKeiver* v. *Pennsylvania*,[28] the Supreme

---

26. Uniform Juvenile Court Act, Nat'l Conf. of Comm. on Uniform States Laws, A.B.A. (1968).
27. Children's Bureau Pub. No. 472 (1969).
28. 402 U.S. 528, 91 S. Ct. 1976, 29 L. Ed. 2d 647 (1971).

Court rejected the contention that a juvenile, like an adult, has a right to a jury trial. It ruled that a jury is not necessary to "fundamental fairness" in a trial of a juvenile and thus is not constitutionally required.[29] The national pace of legal change had perceptibly slowed, but was not reversed.

Today, even in American state courts which have resisted the broad thrust of *Gault*, juveniles are entitled to legal counsel. As this right is ever more generally recognized, attorneys have been appointed in increasing numbers to protect the legal rights of their young clients. Thus, the American juvenile justice system is steadily becoming more of an adversary proceeding like the adult criminal court model. In this transformation much of the promise and nomenclature of the "medical model" juvenile court has been lost or discarded. Today, instead, juveniles are protected against the overzealous and sometimes misguided discretionary actions of judges or social workers imbued with the doctrine of *parens patriae*. If the juvenile court assumes jurisdiction and orders corrective treatment, there are lawyers prepared to demand that promised treatment actually is provided.[30]

As the American juvenile court becomes more of a legal court of last resort where young offenders are adjudicated and sanctions imposed, the question is frequently asked whether it needs to be a separate and independent entity any longer. If the experiences of other nations and cultures is any indication, there is a consensus that the deviance, misbehavior, and crime of the young should be distinguished from adult criminality and

29. Ketchum, *McKeiver v. Pennsylvania: The Last Word in Juvenile Court Adjudications?*, 57 Cornell L. Rev. 561 (1972).

30. Wald & Schwartz, *Trying a Juvenile Right to Treatment Suit: Pointers and Pitfalls for Plaintiffs,* 12 Am. Crim. L. Rev. 125 (1974).

treated separately. The search for an effective system has led in many directions. Sweden and the other Scandinavian countries have chosen a system of child welfare boards to replace courts for children.[31] England and Wales have special panels of lay magistrates,[32] while Scotland has adapted the Swedish experience to a combination of social welfare panels and sheriffs' courts.[33] In Yugoslavia delinquent children under fourteen years of age are supervised and rehabilitated by a social welfare agency, while those fourteen and older are referred to the court system. Latin American procedures for dealing with youthful offenders differ noticeably from the Polish youth system or from the Israeli Juvenile Court. But all seem to agree that a separate juvenile justice system is desirable.[34] Insofar as it represents a common desire to establish an autonomous juvenile justice system, the American experience is universal.

THE DISTINCTIVE ASPECTS OF THE
JUVENILE JUSTICE SYSTEM

When a child or youth acts in a deviant manner, what happens in a typical juvenile justice system? Of course, the very defini-

---

31. Ministry of Justice, *The Child Welfare Act of Sweden* (translated by Thorsten Sellin), Stockholm, 1965; Nyquist, *Juvenile Justice,* in Cambridge Studies in Criminology, St. Martin's (1960).
32. Warburton, *Juvenile Courts in England and Wales,* 16 Int. J. Off. Therapy & Com. Crim. 187 (1972).
33. H. M. Stationery Office, *Social Work (Scotland) Act,* Chapter 49, London (1968); see also Fox, *Juvenile Justice Reforms: Innovations in Scotland,* 12 Am. Crim. L. Rev. 61 (1974).
34. Descriptions of juvenile codes in Belgium, Germany and Switzerland can be found in 17 Int. J. Off. Theapy & Com. Crim. 178, 184 & 189 (1973).

tion of a juvenile varies somewhat from nation to nation and state to state. But it usually means a person less than eighteen years of age. Deviant behavior also has considerable flexiblity of meaning in the statutes of different countries. Universally, it includes those acts which are identified as crimes when committed by anyone, although especially violent or heinous crimes are occasionally excluded. Frequently, it also pertains to a number of acts (such as truancy from school, disobedience toward parents, running away from home, sexual promiscuity, and idleness) which would not be crimes if committed by adults. On occasion it even includes matters over which the child has no control, such as being homeless or parentless, being mentally retarded, or being abused by parents.

However variable the definitions are, a juvenile justice system has three distinct procedures: the prefatory or preadjudication process, the fact-finding or adjudication process, and the rehabilitative or correctional process. When reading about the characteristic features of juvenile justice in different areas of the world in the following chapters, it may be helpful to evaluate and compare them in terms of how each deals with these three main operating features of its system.

THE PREFATORY PROCESS

All juvenile justice philosophy commences with the family relationship. Ordinary deviance or misbehavior of a child is expected to be (and usually is) corrected by parental discipline. In many countries individual parental action is supplemented by private, voluntary community agencies. Parents are encouraged to seek aid from such agencies or to take their errant children to them for initial services. In some of the more structured, sophisticated societies the government has created public social welfare organizations equipped to justify such action. Although such intervention is not entirely a matter of choice by the parent or the child, its responses are couched in helping, rehabilitative terms. Whether such public agencies are considered to be part of the juvenile justice system so as to permit mandatory sanctions depends upon the organizational concepts of the nation that established them.

Further along the spectrum the offending child or youth encounters the policeman or law enforcement agency specifically empowered to deter or arrest persons who break the law or disturb the public order. For most juveniles this is the chief point of entry into the juvenile justice system. But modern police departments also have developed procedures of their own (warnings, station adjustment, traffic schools, and juvenile bureaus) which may permit the juvenile to avoid further contact with the judicial system.

Finally, persistently deviant youth are involuntarily referred by the police to an adjudicatory body—a welfare board or a juvenile court. Thus begins the intake process. In this vestibule of the juvenile justice system two unique features, universal to all juvenile justice systems, are evident. In contrast to an adult, a child at intake is not presumed to have a right to individual freedom pending conviction of a crime. Instead, he or she is entitled only to protective custody and care. Hence, no right to bond or release usually exists. Second, the adjudicatory agency or court asserts a right to choose what cases it will hear. This feature of the intake process is one of the few features of the juvenile justice system which is inherently new, rather than a semantic variation on adult criminal process. When conducted by a skilled intake worker the intake investigation is a highly important turnstile in the system, selecting those youths who are destined to continue through the judgmental system and diverting back into the community many others who will, at most, receive social services.

THE FACT-FINDING ADJUDICATION

Whether it is before a child welfare board or a juvenile court, the case of a youth referred by the police and petitioned after intake screening usually culminates in a fact-finding or adjudicatory hearing. Prior to such a hearing much information concerning the youth's past and current behavior is compiled. In the British and American adversary-style process, with deference to the adage "innocent until proven guilty," preadjudication collection of data is usually limited to proof of prior antisocial acts. But in many other systems it includes mental and physical examinations, educational tests, trial placements, and even the beginning of rehabilitative treatment.

The adjudication process evokes particular concern about safeguarding the legal rights of the child and the parents through due process of law, probably because it closely resembles a trial. Although keen observers of the system might contend that the intake worker's decision is more crucial, in most juvenile justice systems the adjudication hearing is regarded as the day of decision. This is the event which has become the focus for the intervention of attorneys as a consequence of the U.S. Supreme Court's mandate in the *Gault* decision. To these hearings adjudicatory bodies hail the parents, the police, the educators, the social workers, and the complaining witnesses.

Adjudicatory procedures range from the formality of standing in a courtroom before a robed judge to sitting at a relatively informal conference in an agency office. But in all adjudicatory hearings there is a presentation of evidence or testimony to the adjudicating person or group which evaluates it for proof of crime or delinquency. An adjudication thus becomes a fact-finding hearing—as it is sometimes statutorily described. If the proof sustains the allegations of the petition or complaint in whole or in part, the juvenile court or social agency acquires jurisdiction over the youth and proceeds (either immediately or after further social investigation) to a dispositional hearing. If the allegations do not justify continued jurisdiction, the juvenile and his parents are discharged from the system.

THE DISPOSITIONAL OR
POST-ADJUDICATORY PROCESS

After the court or supervisory body acquires jurisdiction, it sets about the correctional or rehabilitative business which has become the hallmark of the juvenile justice system. In countries with a juvenile court system, this usually involves a relatively formal dispositional hearing, not unlike an adult sentencing, at which the judge makes certain major decisions and orders that they be carried out by a social worker, a social agency, or a correctional institution. Most importantly, the juvenile court judge decides whether or not the youth is to be removed from his parents' custody; and, if so, to whose custody he or she will be committed and for how long. Thereafter, the court's order or broad mandate usually is implemented and carried out by a governmental agency outside the legal structure, although probationary services are often an arm of the juvenile court. In nations utilizing social welfare boards, the dispositional process is more gradual because there is less necessity for formal transfer of operating authority after a general assessment or appraisal of the youth's needs are made; the board is frequently an integral part of the social service agency which will carry out the mandate.

The juvenile correctional or rehabilitative process is quite distinguishable from the adult system of penology because it devotes its attention primarily to the social deficiencies of the youth rather than to the type of crime committed—although the latter may in fact shorten or extend the length of ordered supervision. This emphasis upon a disposition that affects the *whole* status and conduct of the offender is a unique characteristic of the juvenile justice system.

The ordered social control may vary widely depending upon the philosophical concepts of the nation, the degree of public concern with the offense involved, and the apparent effectiveness of the behavioral-modification procedure. It can involve punishment, incapacitation, military-like discipline, reeducation, vocational training, psychiatric or medical treatment, restriction of mobility and hours of freedom in the community, loss of privileges, or a change in parental control through substitute parental figures. In a physical sense, this may mean the placement of the youth in a training school, a juvenile reformatory (sometimes called a borstal), a trade school, a hospital, a foster home, a group home, or a halfway house. Many countries also use the principle of suspended sentences. Some exercise the power to order restitution, to require productive labor, or to impose a fine. There is nearly always a system of probation, however rudimentary it may be in some of the less developed countries. In the past, juvenile court systems have often vied among themselves as to the range and variety of their dispositional facilities. But the question most frequently raised today is not the number or variety of the facilities but their efficacy. That, however, is a subject for discussion in the section on current issues set out below.

Also to be considered in the post-adjudication period are the juvenile's legal rights to appeal or review, to petition for modification or release, and subsequently to terminate the supervision and be discharged. There have been far fewer appeals from juvenile court decisions than from comparable adult criminal convictions. But nations that operate juvenile courts usually provide a right of appeal or a mechanism for review of the juvenile courts' fact-finding and dispositional rulings. This is the chief legal postadjudication process in the system.

One of the special features of American and some other juvenile justice systems which distinguishes them from adult criminal law is the concept of continuing jurisdiction. Whereas most criminal courts lose jurisdiction over the criminal after sentencing, a juvenile court continues legally to have responsibility for a juvenile even though he is committed to an institution, a training center, or a foster home.[35] Thus arises another

---

35. A few state statutes follow adult concepts and terminate the local court's jurisdiction when the juvenile is committed to a state-operated institution rather than to community-based or local facilities.

postdispositional feature—the right to petition the original court for review, for modification of its order, or for termination of a commitment. Both lawyers and parents often avail themselves of this right, and the juvenile court is called upon to exercise broad and continuing supervision over the youth it has found to be antisocial or deviant.

Finally, nearly all juvenile justice systems afford a flexible period of control and supervision—an indeterminate sentence or period of probation. This encourages effort, good behavior, and cooperation by the youth in order to obtain early discharge. In many systems indeterminate commitments are customary and discretion is left with the rehabilitative or correctional agency, subject to formal discharge by the court. In other systems the judge plays an active role in deciding when discharge is appropriate. With discharge comes termination of jurisdiction, either immediately or after a test (or parole) period. Nearly all juvenile justice systems include a statutory exhortation that a juvenile's delinquency record shall not be equated with a criminal conviction. This seeks to prevent the type of disenfranchisement, civil penalty, or public stigmatization that an adult criminal conviction often includes. Nevertheless, most observers concede that a record of juvenile delinquency does create a stigma. As a result, in some statutes enacted in the last two decades there are also provisions for the expungement or sealing of a juvenile's record after a year or two of good community behavior. Such procedures after termination tend to minimize any stigma which arises despite hortatory provisions in the law.

THE SOCIAL SIGNIFICANCE OF JUVENILE JUSTICE

While an understanding of the internal operations of various juvenile justice systems is essential to the fullest appraisal of the following chapters, even more important is the external impact of juvenile justice upon the general social order. What is the effect of a juvenile justice system upon a preexisting tribal or family-oriented social system? Have the social mores of a country been bolstered or altered by the impact of its juvenile justice methods? Is the juvenile justice system effective in curbing crime and other antisocial behavior? These are some of the issues raised in the following paragraphs.

Although its velocity has varied from nation to nation, there has been an accelerating pace of change in all societies during the second half of the twentieth century. Some say that such increasing change is the product of historic modificatons of human values; others contend that these human values have been modified by the changing world of today. There is little doubt that an interrelationship exists.

Observers agree that there has been a substantial and constant decline in the authority, the discipline, and the role of the family during this century. Although modern families are frequently cemented by bonds of love and affection, the survival necessities which once made family solidarity a social necessity have been eroded. Discernable factors in the weakening of family ties have been: (1) greater precociousness among boys and girls; (2) impatience with the old and established order; (3) factionalism and accompanying multiplication of life-styles and standards; and finally (4) mounting anxiety which clamors for personal security.

The clientele of the juvenile justice system are children. But the very definition of a child has changed legally and physiologically during the first three quarters of this century. The law's definition of a child usually clings to chronological age for reasons of simplicity and apparent equality of application. Yet the statutory age at which a child becomes an adult varies from state to state and country to country, ranging from fifteen to twenty-one years.[36] Moreover, lawmakers are constantly

---

36. Levin & Sarri, *Juvenile Delinquency: A Comparative Analysis of Legal Codes in the United States,* U. of Michigan Press (1974) p. 13.

debating further alterations of the existing age limit.

Twentieth-century advances in travel, medicine, communications, education, and nutrition have wrought other noticeable modifications. A satellite television transmission from the 1976 Olympic Games indicates the ever increasing physical stature, strength, and athletic prowess of today's youth. World's records are broken ever more regularly, and there seems to be no end in sight. Medical journals suggest that the onslaught of puberty among both male and female children in the United States now occurs at the age of eleven rather than at age fourteen as it did at the beginning of this century.[37] And it is a well- established social fact that girls mature more rapidly than boys between puberty and their eighteenth birthday. These developments all add up to a yeasty, revolutionary ferment in the clientele of the juvenile justice system during this final quarter of the twentieth century.

The end of colonialism throughout the world, the breakdown of African tribal rule, and the disappearance of centuries-old Asian caste systems are but three examples of a growing impatience with the old and established order. As these transitions occur deviance is accepted, even sought after, by those who seek change. And the young who are at least rooted in the old order take on roles of leadership and sometimes resort to violence in order to effect change. Family ties, heritage, and reverence for the past lose their appeal in such a revolutionary milieu.

As the old order crumbles and new horizons emerge, shifting factions vie with each other for preference and dominance. Studies of the French Revolution and the accompanying events throughout Europe and North America in the last quarter of the eighteenth century show a similar pattern. While strongly held,

---

37. Grinder, *Adolescence,* Wiley & Sons (1973) pp. 77-79; Tenner, *Growth at at Adolescence,* Blackwell Scientific Pub. (1962); Young, *Environmental Influences Upon Time of Arrival at Puberty,* 56 R.I. Med. J. 265-273 (1973).

competing policies and standards support differing life-styles, like an amoeba, the body politic repeatedly subdivides. A glance at the membership roster of the United Nations quickly tells us that there are in the world today twice as many nations as existed when that international organization was created a quarter century ago.

In a century that has seen more battle deaths than any previous one and in which two entire cities—Hiroshima and Nagasaki—were destroyed in 1945 by atomic bombs in a matter of seconds, anxiety for personal safety is understandable. But other, more subtle changes have also increased personal tensions. Increasing longevity produced by medical science is not an unmixed blessing. The specter of extended old age without work, family, or the means of life support has generated demands for greater security. So have the pressures of a growing world population threatened with food and water shortages, atmospheric pollution, and a rising level of the oceans. The interaction between growing fears and a clamor for protection from these dangers has created a youthful generation vacillating between fatalistic resignation and a preoccupation with individual security. In this situation family allegiances have not demonstrated an ability to provide the meaning and the security that youth is seeking.

The juvenile justice system is thus an effort to fill the gap caused by the breakdown of natural family control and parental discipline over children. The reasons for the collapse of the family structure will be examined and debated by future historians and social scientists. The fact is that it has faltered. And most of those concerned agree that the family, as a means of social control of the young, is not likely to be reinvigorated under current circumstances. As the renowned Swiss watchmakers of Geneva will tell you, it is not advisable to try to turn the hands of a good clock backward! Hence, either because of the failure of parental control, or because family structure does not assure the social results sought by national governments, juvenile justice systems have been created to replace family control. The state, for better or worse, out of necessity or expedience, has decided to supplant the family as the final arbiter of youthful behavior.

The primary goal of this chapter on perspectives is to delineate those issues, problems, and challenges which are universal and generic to the juvenile justice systems described hereafter so that the reader can assess the future of juvenile justice. But there are two by-products of the establishment of independent systems of justice for juveniles which deserve to be recognized and accepted as having social value and significance of their own:

1. Research Laboratory. Any realistic study of criminal justice will show that judicial and correctional procedure develops rigidity, is subject to obsolescence, and is resistant to modification. It is a factor indigenous to the process. During the past three quarters of a century juvenile justice systems have provided a useful cauldron in which experiments could be tested before transplanting them to an adult system of criminal justice. Rehabilitation, suspended sentences, halfway houses, supervised (or unsupervised) probation, group counseling, intake divergence, consent judgments, indeterminate sentences, and presentence social studies—all of these concepts were either conceived or were extensively applied by juvenile courts before they were adopted for general use in adult criminal justice systems. The juvenile justice system with its greater flexibility provides a useful pilot project for new ideas in the field. With the accelerated pace of change in this century, such a laboratory is of great social value.

2. Preparation for Adulthood. It is also important to sociologists to remember that all juveniles who survive the turbulent age of adolescence become adults by the passage of time. Consequently, the impact of a juvenile justice system upon its youthful clientele has a proximate effect upon most of the adults who may later become involved with adult criminal justice. To

the extent that a juvenile justice system achieves its goals there is a marked decrease in adult criminality. If it fails, greater burdens are placed on the adult criminal justice process. The recognition of this social fact is perhaps one of the reasons why, for the first time, the Fifth United Nations Congress on the Prevention of Crime and Treatment of Offenders scheduled sessions on juvenile justice when it met in Geneva in September 1975.

PREDOMINANT ISSUES AND CURRENT THEMES

Whether a separate, autonomous system of justice for youth is the best way to meet the serious social problem of family breakdown and antisocial behavior by juveniles is frequently asked today. Violent crimes are being committed by juveniles in increasing numbers. To some critics the rehabilitative approach of the treatment model is philosophically wrong because it is permissive. To other, practical-minded observers, the rehabilitative process should be discontinued because it has been unsuccessful. They would discard the juvenile justice system's principles of healing and salvation and allow it to function more like the adult criminal justice model. Whichever motive is adopted, the result would be a juvenile justice system more nearly like the traditional criminal justice pattern. If that path is followed, the question arises whether the juvenile justice system should be reunited with the criminal court structure from which it broke away less than a century ago. Beneath this philosophical discussion there are a number of more specific, administrative issues that recur at national and international conferences concerned with crime and delinquency, such as the Fifth United Nations Congress at Geneva.

LEGAL PROCESS VERSUS SOCIAL WORK
Every nation has established a system for judging the offensive acts (designated "crimes") of one citizen against another. Most nations also have procedures for administering to the sick,

the needy, the crippled, and the blind. But the juvenile justice system with its treatment-oriented, dispositional philosophy has aspects of both the judicial and the social work process. Thus in most countries a constant tension exists between the legal profession, which specializes in rendering judgments, and those who practice social work and the healing arts. The issue is whether the principles of social justice or individual healing should take precedence when there is conflict within the juvenile justice system. In the Scandinavian countries and in Scotland, for example, the judgmental aspect is minimized and legal process takes second place. A "no-fault" approach prevails which diagnoses only the present status of the child, not the moral or legal causes of his antisocial acts. In the United States such a medical model, which largely excluded due process of law, was rejected a decade ago on the ground that in reality the treatment process had never been established. Today the United States is moving steadily toward a juvenile court system controlled by, and responsible to, the legal profession. In still other countries, such as Great Britain, a middle ground has been selected, and effective control is with the lay public through public commissions and citizen magistrates. One of the major issues of this decade will be whether the juvenile justice system should be controlled by law and legal concepts, by behavioral science and social principles, or by the citizen-public in accord with principles of common sense and instinct.

THE SCOPE OF THE COURT'S JURISDICTION

The debate about whether lawyers, social workers, or the lay public should control the juvenile justice system also relates to another current issue: When and to what extent should the state intervene in the lives of juveniles? If intervention is believed to be scientific, beneficial, and rehabilitative, more state action is acceptable than when the intervention is based on fault and the results are judgmental and punitive.

In the United States, the juvenile court process is increasingly dominated by concepts of legal due process. As a result, lawyers drawn into the process are insisting upon explicit procedures set forth in statutory provisions and rules of court. Appellate decisions foster clearly drawn limits of legal jurisdiction and reject as vague subjective standards such as "children growing up in idleness and vice" or "children in need of supervision." Hence, the jurisdiction of the U.S. juvenile court is being narrowed by legal process.

Many social planners in the United States, faced with the reality that juvenile court intervention causes trauma and stigma, also urge statutory amendment to make the juvenile court a social process of last resort. They recommend that minor misbehavior and "status offenses"[38] be eliminated from the juvenile court's jurisdiction to permit it to concentrate on more serious, criminal-like conduct by juveniles. As a consequence, the statutory jurisdiction of some U.S. juvenile courts is being reduced by legislative action.

In contrast—where a social service philosophy prevails—the juvenile justice system increasingly seeks to prevent antisocial offenses by early intervention. In such circumstances the norm is to expand the jurisdiction and extend services to more juveniles. Some of these social efforts are aimed at the entire population of children—such as compulsory educational improvements, more parental counseling, better recreation for youth, and expanded medical services. Other efforts include educational and pyschological testing to detect individual tendencies toward criminality, law enforcement referral of "acting-out" youths to social service agencies, the establishment of youth bureaus for the diver-

---

38. Defined as those acts such as defiance of parental authority, truancy from compulsory schools, running away from home, smoking, drinking, and sexual behavior which are permitted when engaged in by adults but which are prohibited if engaged in by a person who has a legal status as a juvenile. See Status Offenders: A Working Definition, Council of State Governments (1975).

sion of less serious cases, the encouragement of parental referrals, and even placement of nonconforming children. Thus, where social service concepts prevail, the scope of juvenile court intervention tends to grow.

CITIZEN CONTROL AND THE USE OF VOLUNTEERS

Like the political situation in the United Nations itself, within the juvenile justice movement there is a third competing force, mentioned previously: many citizens are disillusioned by the unfulfilled promises of the rehabilitative type of juvenile justice system and yet do not wish it to become judgmental. They do not want it run by either the legal or the social work profession but prefer that lay people control and guide the process, calling upon professionals only as consultants. This group advocates local citizens' councils, lay magistrates, and greater use of voluntary social agencies and volunteers. They believe that the juvenile justice system should be directed by lay persons not professionals.

THE PROBLEM OF ABUSED AND
NEGLECTED CHILDREN

One problem of this decade which seems common to all juvenile justice systems, whether administered by lawyers, social workers, or citizens, is the rising number of seriously neglected or physically abused children.[39] Both medical and legal researchers are concerned and have taken additional measures to discover such children and provide appropriate care and protection for them. Society's response toward a parent who abuses his or her child varies widely—from anger and punitive action to pity and treatment. Many believe that retributive action against an abusing parent only compounds the child's plight. A recent

---

39. See McCord, *The Battered Child, Part I,* 50 Minn. L. Rev. 1 (1965); Paulsen, *Child Abuse Reporting Laws,* 67 Col. L. Rev. 1 (1967).

response to this growing problem has been legislation in some U.S. states transferring jurisdiction over such adult criminal conduct to a juvenile court if the person charged (juvenile or adult) is a member of the same family as the victim. Such intra-family offense jurisdiction may prove a valuable tool in preventing children from being abused or neglected within their families. A corollary of this heightened awareness of neglected and abused children is the establishment of a family court where a multitude of family problems—delinquency, neglect, paternity of illegitimate children, adoption, mental illness, and retardation—are all considered by the same judge or government agency. The family court concept is largely a product of post–World War II social planning and has grown slowly.[40] But it seems likely that the plight of abused and neglected children will be given greater emphasis in the policies of juvenile justice systems in the decade ahead.

INDIVIDUAL RIGHTS FOR CHILDREN

Until the twentieth century children were numbered among a man's assets and as such were regarded as a special form of property or chattel. In this century, as this attitude has changed the individuality and personhood of a child has been recognized, and with this recognition has come the slow and halting growth

---

40. Alexander, *The Family Court: An Obstacle Race?,* 19 U. Pitt. L. Rev. 602 (1963); Arthur, *A Family Court—Why Not?,* 51 Minn. L. Rev. 233 (1966); Dyson & Dyson, *Family Courts in the United States,* 8 J. Fam. L. 507 (1968); H. M. Stationery Office, *The Child, the Family and the Young Offender* (British White Paper) London (1966) and comments in 6 British J. of Crim. No. 2 (1966); Law Reform Commission of Canada, *The Family Court: Working Paper No. 1* (1974); General Secretariat, Supreme Court of Japan, *Eighteen Years of the Family Courts of Japan* (1968).

of individual rights for children. In 1948 the United Nations adopted the Universal Declaration of Human Rights[41] applicable to all persons. In addition, the United Nations has proclaimed a Third Declaration of the Rights of the Child,[42] which calls for the special protection and entitlements deemed necessary for childhood. These rights guarantee a child food and shelter, nurture, care and custody, education, and eventual emancipation. They are worthy human goals not yet fully achieved in most countries, but progress toward them has improved the status of children in many nations.

In the nations where legal process controls the juvenile justice system, both courts and lawmakers during the past two decades have enunciated a series of personal legal rights which protect children.[43] For example, as described above, the Supreme Court of the United States has declared that a child charged with a legal offense for which he or she can be incarcerated is entitled: (1) to legal counsel; (2) to a detailed written statement of the charges; (3) to confront accusers who must testify under oath and submit to cross-examination; (4) to refuse to testify about the alleged offense; (5) to have the charge established beyond a reasonable doubt; and (6) to be entitled to appellate review of the trial. Many more details surrounding these basic rights have evolved through the decisions of state appellate courts or by statutory amendments to state juvenile court acts.

The assertion of a child's individual rights should accelerate in

----

41. UN General Assembly, Paris (1948). See special issue of Journal of International Comm. of Jurists commemorating International Year for Human Rights (1968).
42. UN General Assembly, New York (October 1959). See 22 International Child Welfare Rev. 4-8 (1968).
43. Klapmuts, *Children's Rights,* 4 Crime & Delinquency Literature No. 3 (1972); See Foster & Freed, *A Bill of Rights for Children,* 6 Fam. L. Q. 343 (1972).

the decade ahead because the prevailing attitude toward children has changed markedly since the turn of the century. The Old Testament set forth various grounds upon which a father could put his son to death. No longer is such absolute parental authority accepted. Even the milder Victorian concept that "Father knows best" is disappearing. Instead, a populist belief in participatory democracy has arisen that seems to include children—at least those who have reached puberty. By the latest version of a model juvenile court act, a child in the United States would be given the right to file an action on his own behalf against a parent, school, welfare agency, rehabilitative institution, or other governmental agency, if necessary to protect his individual rights.[44] The extent and nature of such new rights for children and youth will be a major topic of discussion at future meetings of those concerned with juvenile justice.

THE RIGHT TO TREATMENT AND THE
LIMITS OF BEHAVIORAL SCIENCE

Many juvenile justice systems in the early years of this century adopted a medical model of operation, that is, a child was to be treated according to a doctor's diagnosis of his behavioral disorder. Such a philosophy was so persuasive—both for its noble motivation and for its analogy—that it went unchallenged for many years. Until World War II there was an exuberant belief that human behavior was infinitely modifiable—that there was "no such thing as a bad boy," that any person who was mentally ill was curable, and that education and wholesome employment would "set right" a delinquent youth. But the disappointments and failures in mental health treatment and behavioral modification of the past three decades have caused a

---

44. Section 8 (4) of 1974 Draft of Seventh Edition of Standard Juvenile Court Act prepared by the Council of Judges to the National Council on Crime and Delinquency.

sharp deterioration of public trust in behavioral science and its ability to provide ordered treatment.[45] Today the qualifications of the "doctor," the scientific validity of the "diagnosis," and the ability to prescribe treatment for the "disorder" are all being challenged.

Many question whether present-day knowledge of human behavior is capable of the rehabilitation promised. There are also those who contend that diagnoses being made by judges and others untrained in behavioral science are more concerned with law enforcement than with behavioral science. Such critics recommend that future treatment dispositions be made by boards of social scientists after a juvenile court judge has decided the facts. At least this would insure that the treatment ordered would be designed to meet the juvenile's needs.

But even when appropriate treatment does exist and is ordered, the delivery of services to juveniles is often faulty. Consequently, there are frequent legal and social efforts to have a court mandate treatment. In furtherance of this purpose, in 1974 the Council of Judges to the National Council on Crime and Delinquency drafted the following definition of the right to treatment:

> After a child is adjudicated and found by a juvenile court to be within its jurisdiction, the court shall hold a disposition hearing and issue an order of disposition providing for custody, guidance, care and discipline that will meet the remedial needs of the child. If the parent, guardian or custodian to whom the court releases the child by its order of disposition, or the person, agency or institution to whose

---

45. Report of the Commission on Mental Health Services, Family Court of the City of New York, *Juvenile Justice Confounded, Pretensions and Realities of Treatment Services* (1972).

custody the court commits the child by its order of disposition, fails to provide any special care, treatment or services required by the court's order of disposition, the child, his attorney, or the person retaining residual parental rights may petition the court to either implement the order of disposition or discharge the child. If, following a judicial hearing on such petition, the court finds that the child has failed to receive ordered care, treatment or services, it shall either issue such further order as is necessary to implement the original order, or modify or revoke the order. Unavailability of facilities or services shall not be accepted by the court as grounds for denying the petition, but refusal by the child to accept or to cooperate in ordered care or treatment may be considered by the court. Unless the court is able to mandate the requisite care, treatment or services appropriate to the child's remedial needs, it shall release the child to the custody of his or her parent, guardian or custodian with or without conditions of probation or supervision, *provided however* that, if it is established at a judicial hearing that said child would be a clear and present danger to the community's safety if released, the court may order such custody and supervision as is necessary to ensure the community's safety.[46]

Indications are that such a right to treatment will place a correlative duty upon the juvenile justice system to require that the treatment reality for children substantially conforms to the rehabilitative promises that have justified many dispositional orders in the past.[47]

------

46. Section 24 of 1974 Draft of Seventh Edition of Standard Juvenile Court Act prepared by the Council of Judges to the National Council on Crime and Delinquency.
47. Pyfer, *The Juvenile's Right to Treatment,* 6 Fam.L.Q. 279 (1972).

INSTITUTIONS VERSUS COMMUNITY-BASED
FACILITIES

Any study of treatment leads to an examination of the facilities which are expected to deliver these social services. For several decades leaders of the juvenile court movement have decried their lack of financial support and the resulting inadequacy and insufficiency of the facilities and supporting services necessary to correct and rehabilitate delinquent youth. In fact, the most frequent retort to detractors of the juvenile justice system has been that it would succeed if given a fair trial with sufficient resources and facilities.[48]

But evaluation of the type of large institution most often used for committed juveniles repeatedly has found them wanting. They are excessively expensive to operate, out of touch with urban culture from which their clients come and to which they will return, counterproductive in the deterrence of future crime, and destructive of any vestiges of independence or self-reliance existing in the delinquent youth assigned to them.[49] If behavioral science can positively change and improve the conduct of delinquent youth, a typical juvenile training school or youth reformatory is not the place to do it. Whether at the juvenile or the adult level, present-day penologists seem ready to concede that the mass institution housing hundreds of prisoners is a failure as

---

48. Polier, *A View from the Bench, The Juvenile Court,* N.C.C.D. (1964) pp. 1-86; Young, *Is the Juvenile Court Successful?,* 22 Juv. Ct. J. 55 (1971); Edwards, *In Defense of the Juvenile Court,* 23 Juvenile Justice No. 2 (1972) pp. 2-6; Polier, *The Future of the Juvenile Court,* 26 Juvenile Justice No. 2 (1975) pp. 3-10.
49. *Corrections in the United States, Chapter 3, Juvenile Institutions,* 13 Crime and Delinquency 73-96 (1967); National Council on Crime and Delinquency, *The Nondangerous Offender Should Not Be Imprisoned* (Policy Statement) 1973.

a rehabilitative tool. Protection of the community may justify the incarceration in secure institutions of those persons— juvenile or adult—who are a clear and present danger to their fellow citizens. But the use of fortress institutions should be limited to incapacitation of the relatively few dangerous convicts rather than used for the rehabilitation of the average lawbreaker.

Much greater hope of rehabilitation can be found among the variety of community-based facilities that have sprung up wherever juvenile justice systems are alert and probing for new solutions. The nature and style of such facilities for the delivery of services are too numerous to catalogue. Some are residences called semi-libertes or halfway houses; some are group homes or pensions; others are outpatient clinics or daytime training pro- grams. By definition, they are situated in the community where the person served is living; most of them are small; and emphasis and expenditure is on the delivery of needed services rather than on incarceration, care, or custody. The data are not all collected on their ability to effect permanent change, but there is little doubt that they are more humane, less costly, and avoid many of the demonstrated faults of large juvenile institutions.

---

50. U.S. Government Print Office (1967).
51. 7 Crime and Delinquency, 97, 109, N.C.C.D. (1961).

3

Prevention and Diversion in the United States

Frederick Ward, Jr.

In the United States programs designed to prevent delinquency and efforts to assist offenders by diverting them to programs and services outside the juvenile justice system in the hope of reducing the repetition of delinquency are not new.

The concept of delinquency prevention is at least as old as the definition of delinquency itself; and the ancient adage, "An ounce of prevention is worth a pound of cure," appeals to our common sense in this as well as in most other areas of human concern. Accordingly, a plethora of special programs, along with almost all public and private health, education, and welfare services for youth, lay claim to the idea that they can and do prevent juvenile delinquency.

Diversion of children from the judicial process is also an old concept. In the United States around the turn of the century, the juvenile court movement itself was a strategy for "rescuing" children from the harsh proceedings and punishment of the criminal court by diverting them to the more humanitarian and protective environment of the juvenile court, which would be more concerned with the individual than with the particular offense. In turn, diversion from the juvenile court of certain children has always been exercised through the discretion of police officers, probation officers, and even judges.

The terms "prevention" and "diversion" are frequently used interchangeably, since programs to which youngsters may be referred outside the juvenile justice system, whether designed for all children or only for those with special problems, are presumed to prevent further delinquent behavior. Recreation programs, child guidance, special school counseling, special education, youth employment, child and family services are examples of such programs.

The term "diversion" has many meanings, and within the system of juvenile justice it is frequently used to describe the assignment of offenders to less restrictive alternatives; for example, diversion from a youth institution to a foster home or open group home, diversion to "unofficial" probation or to a special caseload, and so on.

An additional problem with the term "prevention" is that the raison d'etre of each element of the juvenile justice system—police, courts, detention, probation, institutions—includes the idea of prevention; prevention of delinquency through deterrence, prevention of further delinquency on the part of individual offenders through corrections, prevention of delinquency through police visibility, and so on.

Clearly, a standard set of definitions for prevention and diversion is called for, and several attempts have been made to accomplish this. Lejins[1] has identified three types of prevention: punitive (threat of punishment will deter others); correction (eliminating causes); and mechanical (placing obstacles, such as street lighting, police surveillance, etc.). In this scheme, most of the programs to which children are diverted would be found in

---

1.   P. Lejins, "The Field of Prevention," *Delinquency Prevention,* Amos and Wellford, Ed. Prentice Hall, Englewood Cliffs, N.J. 1967.

the second classification. Others[2] have suggested an adaptation of the medical model, which also uses three classifications: primary prevention (modification or removal of delinquency-producing conditions); secondary prevention (early identification and intervention); and tertiary prevention (strategies to prevent recidivism through rehabilitation). The last[3] would seem to be a goal of correctional agencies as well as of most diversion programs.

For purposes of identification and evaluation, there is a need to view separately efforts which promote the general welfare of children (prevention) from nonjudicial, preadjudicatory alternatives to which children whose behavior can be described as delinquent are referred (diversion). Standards for diversion programs as well as for practices of referral out of the juvenile justice system are presently lacking.

Today, in the United States both diversion and prevention are being given added emphasis due not only to the rising volume of juvenile arrests but also because of the reexamination of the role of juvenile and family courts with respect to noncriminal and minor cases of delinquency where nonjudicial alternatives would not only seem to be more effective but more appropriate and less harmful.

The destructive effects of detention and institutionalization for nondangerous children, most of whom have committed no criminal act (under circumstances often injurious to their mental and emotional health and sometimes to their physical safety), has aroused interest and concern nationally in reform. At the same time, the juvenile court is being criticized for not dealing

---

2. Paul J. Brantingham, and Frederic L. Faust, "The Conceptive Model of Crime Prevention," *Crime and Delinquency,* NCCD, Hackensack, N.J. July 1976.
3. U.S. National Criminal Justice Information Statistics Service, *Children in Custody,* p. 6.

more adequately with the serious delinquent, with the result that provisions for lowering the age of jurisdiction and the age at which children may be waived to the adult criminal court for trial are being proposed in many jurisdictions.

Therefore, diversion and prevention are also supported as strategies for relieving the juvenile court of an unnecessary volume of cases so that it will be able to concentrate its efforts on those involving serious delinquency.

In this regard, there is a strong movement in the United States to remove child "status offenses" from the jurisdiction of the juvenile court. These are offenses applicable only to children that would not be crimes if committed by adults; for example, truancy, running away from home, curfew violations, waywardness, incorrigibility, and so on—situations which in the Scandinavian countries are the responsibility of child welfare councils and in a number of other countries are the responsibility of the school system or nonjudicial agencies concerned with minors.

A few years ago, in order to avoid labeling such children as delinquent, about half of the states in the United States provided a new label, giving rise to a curious collection of acronyms such as PINS (person in need of supervision); CINS (children in need of supervision); JINS (juveniles in need of supervision); and now even FINS (families in need of supervision).

However, recent studies indicate that despite the nondelinquent status accorded "children in need of supervision," from 25 to 40 percent of the boys and some 70 percent of the girls in jails, detention homes, and correctional institutions are in this category. Also, they report that such children generally remain longer in institutions than those committed for acts of delinquency. Awareness of this anomaly has recently motivated almost one-third of the states (sixteen) to prohibit institutionalization in such cases, and the federal government has appropriated funds to enable the diversion of such children from the system and to prevent their future placement in institutions.

While the major outcry has been for the removal and diversion of status offenders out of the system, diversion is seen also as an alternative for many nondangerous delinquent children. Not that diversion of many such children has not been practiced by the juvenile justice system since its inception—in fact, most of the children who come to the attention of police and juvenile court authorities, at least in the first instance, can be said to be diverted, if by that we mean referral to a community agency or dismissed with a warning. The problem has been too little follow-up by the referring agent and little follow-through by youngsters or their parents.

Also, the absence of adequate referral procedures and the lack of community resources for helping troubled children are seen as factors affecting the increased volume of juveniles being accepted into the system. However, many if not most judges resist losing jurisdiction of status offenses, claiming that community services are either not available or refuse to accept troublesome, acting-out children.

Others point out that the juvenile court, by accepting the responsibility and relieving parents, schools, and the community of such children, has served to inhibit the development of other alternatives.

The current call for greater use of diversion is also viewed as a part of a general movement toward broader social reform which would reduce alienation and racism and increase economic and social opportunity for those who are most likely to be brought into the system of juvenile and criminal justice: the young, the poor, and members of minority groups.

Although we have no hard data on the present use of diversion, it is generally conceded that the volume is increasing and will be further stimulated by provisions of the Juvenile Justice and Delinquency Prevention Act, which will stimulate state and local programs of prevention and diversion as part of a broad nationwide program of community-based alternatives to juvenile institutions and detention facilities.

47

Because of the force of the legislation and the anticipated increase in available funds, it is expected that diversion will continue as a national trend in the United States for some time to come and that once diversion becomes institutionalized as a major strategy of juvenile justice the structures and means now lacking in most communities and states will probably be developed.

The practice of diversion builds on the use of inherent as well as statutory discretion by police and probation authorities. In this regard, special police and probation screening and referral units, as now practiced in several major cities, are viewed as possible models for attaining a more systematic process for the selection of children for diversion. It is generally conceded that diversion should be noncoercive and that the relationship between the child and receiving agency should be voluntary. Otherwise we are likely to exchange the "laws delay and insolence of office" for administrative tyranny.

The types and varieties of special programs to which children are now being diverted are too numerous to describe. However, they include programs of special education, group work, casework, guided group interaction, skill training, employment, use of volunteers, family counseling, and the like. Most of these are remedial programs and proceed along traditional lines, generally without evaluation and with uncertain results.

As important as diversion may be to the individual who otherwise may be detained, placed on probation, or committed to an institution, the effects of diversion on rates of delinquency, or on the juvenile justice system itself, is open to question if we consider Durkeim's theory of stable levels of crime and Blumstein's thesis that society tends to impose a fairly constant level of punishment.[4] Other evidence seems to suggest that social

---

4.   Alfred Blumstein, and Jacqueline Cohen, "A theory of the stability of punishment," *Journal of Criminal Law and Criminology* (Chicago), 64 (2): 198-207, 1973.

forces keep commitment rates within identifiable upper and lower levels.[5] Anttila, in discussing this phenomenon, explains that crime and punishment are in social balance that has an inner logic of its own that does not allow for diversion to go too far and does not permit the number of criminal laws, crimes, and criminals to fall below a certain level.[6]

It would seem, therefore, that we are faced with a thermostat effect. As diversion lowers the number going through the system, other social forces will cause the thermostat to open, enabling admissions to rise again. This may explain the conflicting trends in the United States which seem to be pushing in two directions at once: diversion on one hand and demands for harsh punishment on the other. If these theories are correct, then prevention rather than diversion would seem to offer the best long-run solution.

However, the choice of prevention strategy depends on how we view delinquency. In the absence of good evaluation information and a clear understanding of delinquency causation, programs and projects are usually developed and perpetuated on the basis of myth and faith.

A recent examination of 6,600 studies of delinquencyprevention programs, of which only ninety-five contained some empirical data, concluded that certain types of projects fail to show any evidence of effectiveness; among these are recreation programs, guided group interaction, social casework, and detached gang-worker projects. However, the evidence suggested that

---

5. Lowell L. Kuehn, *An evaluation of the California Probation Subsidy Program.* Ann Arbor, Mich., University Microfilms, 1973. 209 pp. (Dissertation).

6. Inkeri Anttila, "Conservative and Radical Criminal Policy in the Nordic Countries," in *Scandinavian Studies in Criminology,* vol. 3. Oslo, Universitetsforlaget, 1971, pp. 9-21.

other approaches, such as volunteers, youth service bureaus, and special school projects, do hold some promise for success.[7]

These findings suggest that more positive results could be obtained if delinquency prevention is approached from a problem-solving perspective rather than from a medical and moral perspective in which the delinquent is viewed as being in need of reform, treatment, or punishment.

Youth service bureaus, familiarly known in the United States as YSBs, are generally conceded to offer some promise as a community structure through which the needs of youth generally can be met. The YSB, as recommended by the National Council on Crime and Delinquency, fulfills an advocacy role on behalf of youth, works for systems change in their interest, and involves youth and adults in helping create conditions which promote the best interests of young people. It does not provide direct service except on a demonstration basis.[8] The YSB movement within the past five years has spread to some three hundred communities, which would seem to be symptomatic of an "idea whose time has come." But whether through the structure of the YSB or in some other form, the beginning of a more systematic approach to delinquency prevention seems to be under way.

If so, this will have consequences for the future role of the juvenile court as well as for services for adjudged delinquents. In the future, the court may play a supporting role by mandating services for children, institutions may be needed for very few

_____

7. Michael C. Dixon, and William E. Wright, *Juvenile Delinquency Prevention Programs: An Evaluation of Policy Related Research on the Effectiveness of Prevention Programs,* Nashville, Tenn., Peabody College for Teachers, 1975. 2 pts.

8. Sherwood Norman, *The Youth Service Bureau—A Key to Delinquency Prevention,* Hackensack, N.J. National Council on Crime and Delinquency, 1973. 244 pp.

children, and juvenile probation workers may become advocates and community-change agents.

But the most important consequence may be in the changing roles of youth themselves. For as we develop a higher sense of the value and worth of all children and youth in our society and open ways for their participation in the search for solutions to problems which affect them and their future, then we will see them as resources rather than as problems.

To the extent that such participation promises to become a practice, prevention promises to become a reality.

4

Strategies for the Future of Juvenile Corrections

Milton Luger

Correction's problems are manifold; its potential is great. If we are thinking of the future and what directions we should be moving toward, it would be helpful to sketch the present juvenile system to be found in so many places. Juvenile correction is the stepchild of a multiproblem family, located at the end of a supposed continuum of services for children and young people in trouble with themselves and with the law. Correction is the recipient of everyone else's failures. Often after the family, the neighborhood, the schools, the mental health and social welfare officials have had their turn at attempting to make youngsters conforming, obedient, grateful, and productive young citizens, the juvenile justice system is called upon to instill the respect, insight, and cooperativeness which everyone else had failed to achieve. But it is hard to clean smoke-damaged garments, especially if the intent is to dispose of them through a cheap basement sale at bargain rates. It is equally naive to think that, with the present state of knowledge of human dynamics and juvenile correction's inability to control or manipulate all the variables which have an impact upon the successful reintegration of young, troubled people into societal productivity, this can be accomplished by merely being offered limitless funds.

What I am implying here is that the juvenile justice and, especially, the correctional system, has been starved for funds; but this is a poor excuse for those in the system who wring their hands and lament about how much they could do if they only had the money. The malaise that is sickening juvenile corrections is deeper than the lack of fiscal resources and quickly adding huge amounts of funds would probably be wasteful. I believe we must start earlier and with a different tack, if we want to make a meaningful impact on the problem.

CORRECTION'S SECOND-CLASS CITIZEN ATTITUDES

What pervades the field on the part of those who are given the responsibility of administering juvenile correction programs is a second-class-citizen attitude and a belief that they are entitled to little, that they are expected to work miracles in impossible situations, that they are neither respected nor worthy, that their mission is to keep unwanted and unloved young people from bothering a society that has reached its frustration and tolerance levels as far as youth behavior is concerned. Many others who attempted to work with these same children and who damaged them more than helped them in their contacts with them, now perhaps as an ego-saving mechanism, view juvenile correction personnel with condescension and disrespect. These referral sources to the juvenile correction field rationalize their actions usually by stating that their own responsibilities are to the broader population which is more amenable to treatment and guidance. This is usually a euphemism to describe those youth who are willing to ingest the pap offered by most societal institutions and to regurgitate the expected, conforming answers. Not to do so is to incur the wrath of community leaders and to be banished, after many threats, to the correctional establishment. This is usually accompanied by public announcements that the leper colony of juvenile correction will only further infect the diseased individuals, but at least they will not in turn infect others. Correction workers, with their poor self-image and lack of self-worth, are hardly in a position to assist those who are sent to them because they, too, have the same feelings about themselves. And so the rejected are to be controlled, understood, and perhaps treated by those who feel rejected. The goal becomes the avoidance of untoward embarrassing incidents rather than the alleviation of youthful anguish or hostility.

The situation is further aggravated by the fact that the poor and the minority groups find their way to public correctional institutions in disproportionate numbers, and are handled by staff mainly comprised of individuals composed of other ethnic and economic classes. In this time of heightened ethnic awareness, feelings of polarization, suspicion, and mistrust are infused into the milieu of correctional institutions and processes. Traditionally, institutions have been removed from the offenders' communities and a conscientious, enlightened administrator would have difficulty in recruiting minority group staff even if he were inclined to do so. Not only is distance a problem, but civil service tradition and bureaucratic procedures aggravate the situation and block his efforts. Culturally biased paper-and-pencil tests often preclude the large-scale recruitment and certainly the promotion of minority-group staff who could relate well to disadvantaged delinquents.

Employee concerns about fringe benefits of the job too often result in a focus on such issues as seniority as related to preferred assignments and pass days rather than on the meeting of youth needs or the making available of sensitive staff to youths at the times and places that they are required.

The results, too often, are the procedures and policies which fall at the extremes of child-care practices. Youths are handled in a rigid, mechanistic fashion which emphasizes conformity and order; or they are, through fear and ignorance on the part of shaky staff members, cajoled through ultrapermissiveness which is rationalized as "caring" and "nonpunitive" by staff but is interpreted as "uninvolved" and "uninterested" by youths.

Because correction itself feels that it makes no worthy tradition or contribution, its personnel attempt to borrow from other fields to gain community acceptance and to attempt to establish itself as a profession. For example, institutional social workers and probation and parole officers cling to the naive notion that what is wrong with the bulk of these angry, troubled youths can be remedied through adopting the medical model utilized by mental health practitioners. They do not perceive that these approaches, possibly helpful with middle-class, anxious, neurotic youths, have little impact upon the majority of the youngsters who are sent to public institutions and who are not grateful for the proffered treatment. Correction's focus is too often upon trying to emulate the credentialed therapy hour rather than upon attempts to create a helping and hopeful milieu in which the youngster can be stabilized. Instead of giving youngsters responsibility and chances to mature through making decisions, the correctional system tends to infantilize them and implies to them that, if they are compliant, conform, and heed advice, they shall become well. What is not spelled out is what all this has to do with youths' substandard housing, irrelevant community education, unconscionable unemployment rates, pathological parents, stigmatizing welfare systems, and other realities of the communities to which they will be returning briefly. This is all done as we decide what is right for the youth rather than what the youths' rights are. From the tradition of *parens patriae* has evolved unilateral and arbitrary determinations on the part of adults as to what and how young delinquents and other troubled youths shall be handled.

The foregoing is, of course, generalized, and I would be the first to acknowledge that many, many industrious and well-intentioned individuals are laboring in the field of juvenile correction with the hope of making young peoples' lives less troublesome and more productive. They care about, and even in the best sense, love these seemingly unlovable children. But staff has become increasingly ground down, cynical, embittered, and frustrated to the point of becoming defensive. They cannot distinguish between an inadequate system (or better yet, "non-system") and feeling that *they* are being called inadequate, and so they rise to defend their antiquated approaches, cover their covert fears, and resist the risk of introspection which might result in more innovation.

All this does not seem to hold much promise for change. Yet, I believe that if we do not settle for gimmickry or easy panaceas or attempt to achieve the impossible, juvenile correction has a high potential for becoming a source of help and encouragement to youngsters who desperately need the guidance, encouragement, and support which other segments of our societal institutions have neglected to offer them. There are basic things that need to be understood and basic approaches that must be implemented. Some of these, which follow, might seem obvious and trite, but we too often take them for granted as being in operation while we strive to announce our model demonstration projects to the media; these new approaches can never succeed because we are building them on the quicksand of past disillusionment and cynicism.

A YOUTH PUBLIC POLICY

This nation has not enunciated a uniform, assertive public policy position about young people. There has been more rhetoric than substance stated in our pronouncements that "youth is our most precious resource." The uncoordinated, fragmented panoply of federally funded programs in the area of delinquency prevention and treatment is one testimony to our interest in empires, turfs, and bureaucracies rather than in mounting practical, cost-effective approaches toward positive youth development. The new Juvenile Justice Act mandates an analysis of the sundry, disparate federal approaches in this area with the goal in mind of better coordination and communication on all levels. The federal administration must supply fiscal assistance to localities as well as cooperatively setting standards of programming in order to encourage beneficial endeavors on behalf of young people.

What we also need is a loud, determined, and sustained pronouncement from the highest executive and legislative body in each state that they are interested in juvenile corrections. They must, through visitation and through the media, make personal contacts with both staff and youth, and exhibit concern. Staff too often have been subjected to elected officials and legislators arriving at their institutions with an entourage of reporters and TV cameras either after some untoward incident has occurred or at election time. The personal visitation during untroubled and nonelection times of key officials to juvenile facilities will be invaluable in enhancing the self-image and feelings of worth on the part of both staff and youths. The message to the juvenile correction system must be that there is recognition of the difficulty of its mandate. It must be made clear that the major goal of juvenile correction is not to prevent abscondences. It must be impressed upon correctional staff that they will be supported should untoward incidents occur as long as their risk-taking is involved with innovative programming and honest practical attempts to improve youths in rehabilitative endeavors.

At the same time the staff is being "freed up" to work *with* instead of merely to *watch* youngsters, the strategy must include a call to the conscience of the general public as to their responsibility for providing resources and opportunities to involve youths in meaningful activities. Rehabilitation can never occur solely in institutions. The genesis of much of the troublesome behavior on the part of young people is in the dysfunctioning of sundry societal institutions and mechanisms. Therefore, the responsibility to alter and adapt these institutions to help resolve problem behavior must be recognized. Civic groups such as League of Women Voters, National Council of Jewish Women, Jaycees, Chambers of Commerce, Urban League, statewide PTAs, and so on, can be urged to focus upon juvenile delinquency as an objective for their local chapters' programming. This has, of course, been done in the past, but the governor's and legislators' personal intervention and leadership would be of vital importance here. By stressing community responsibility, the door is open for local involvement in neighborhoods for programs such as work-and-study release, group homes, sheltered workshops, volunteer activities, and so on. Concomitantly, there needs to be a shift in the perception of correctional workers, such as parole and aftercare workers, from the notion that they are the youths' caseworkers, to the concept that they are, along with the youth and their families, part of a community advocate approach.

It makes little sense to counsel a youth about his shortcomings and need to change when there are so many things that are wrong with his own community which makes him feel that his future is bleak and his prospects hopeless. There is some reality and much rationalization on the part of older adolescents that they, along with their older brothers, are victims of political persecution and therefore have no right to be trapped in the juvenile justice system at all. By adorning themselves in political-prisoner garb, they can espouse persuasive reasons for their antisocial and illegal activities. One of the ways that correction personnel can help to cut through their arguments is to convince young people that they, too, want to change the social conditions and neighborhoods that breed hostility. Thus, for exam ple, aftercare workers can spend less time in moralizing or threatening youths about not reporting for appointments and more time in neighborhoods with youths conducting block parties, clothing drives, organizing recreation leagues, participating in community school boards, and so on. Many societal institutions such as schools and mental health facilities are undergoing dynamic changes as they move toward more and more community control. This movement holds much promise for the correctional field if it is handled sensitively and sensibly instead of resisted by the correctional establishment. Communities are increasingly demanding that they have more power to make determinations and decisions in connection with mental health services, school programs, drug clinics, and the like, and representation on local boards as evidence of their growing desire to "take care of their own."

The reason that middle-class children are generally not institutionalized in public facilities is that the middle class has organized resources to divert troublesome children from the juvenile justice system. When lower-class parents feel, with public tax dollars, that they can determine the nature of local services, they will be more in a position to place pressure upon local groups to create relevant resources to serve their children, rather than helplessly seeing them shipped off to far-off, mass congregate training schools.

The involvement as a community and youth advocate may bring some criticism to the correctional worker if he and his clients are perceived as challenging the functioning of other bureaucracies. This is another area in which the governor and the legislature may play a key role. They must make it patently clear to other agencies over which they exercise fiscal control, such as welfare and mental hygiene departments, that they expect no policies to be followed which tend to exclude groups of youngsters from services. An example of this is the defective delinquent or the severely emotionally disturbed youngster who is constantly shuttled back and forth between the hospital and the juvenile institution, as both claim they cannot serve this type of youngster. Not only must responsibility for services be pinpointed within each agency, but who will take an active role in cooperating with community groups as more and more programming becomes community-based must be settled.

DIVERSION VERSUS SCREENING OUT

This raises the entire issue of diversion from the juvenile justice system. It is popular today to advocate minimal penetration and maximum diversion of as many juveniles as possible in order to avoid labeling and stigmatizing procedures which later plague the youngster. The argument follows that legal records, no matter how confidential they are supposed to be, have a way of being made available to school systems, to prospective employers, and to others who later come in contact with children. This not only sets up discriminatory practices which work against the youngsters' reintegration and rehabilitation but encourges the self-fulfilling prophecy of continued delinquent involvement. It cannot reasonably be advocated that more children should be handled through the present overworked juvenile courts. As a matter of fact, there is much movement afoot to legislate the screening out of status offenders such as incorrigibles, truants, and so on, from the juvenile justice system entirely, so that they cannot be institutionalized in the same facilities in which delinquent youngsters are handled.

This is a seemingly attractive stance to adopt, but there are dangers inherent in this position as well which must be recognized and for which planning is vital. For example, in some states there are not-too-subtle procedures through which, despite their acts, minority-group children tend to be adjudicated as delinquents, while others youths, for similar acts, tend to be adjudicated as PINS, CINS, CHINS, or whatever the state calls its status offenders. If the argument is followed that status offenders cannot be handled through the juvenile court or treated in institutions handling juvenile delinquents, will this, in the long run, make for racially segregated institutions? In one state, a recent survey indicated that about 90 percent of status offenders had indeed perpetrated delinquent acts, but the judges still adjudicated them as CINS. The training schools in that state attempted to separate CINS from juvenile delinquents, and racial segregation was rampant. Furthermore, as we move toward more and more community-based programming such as urban homes and the like, might the community's resistance to these facilities be stiffened if it felt that only delinquent and principally minority-group youths would be programmed there?

61

Does this approach write off and condemn those youngsters who *do* end up institutionalized to far-off training schools, and does this approach further convince these youngsters of their worthlessness? If we follow this route, will fewer resources be made available for correctional institutions, as the public begins to believe that only delinquent youngsters are processed by the juvenile courts? And what assurances do we have that the other societal institutions, which previously failed the incorrigible-status offenders and truants, will change their bureaucratic practices so that they can offer more relevant and responsible services to these difficult children?

Might it be better to acknowledge that the enormous societal institutions such as schools, mental health services, and so on will always have some fallout, and that it is necessary to support and enhance the image of a manageable entity such as juvenile correction rather than putting all of the community's hopes on making the mammoth societal institutions so relevant that they will have no fallout? What is advocated here is not for more youngsters to be sent to the juvenile justice system, but for public administrators to face up honestly to the problem of what organizational structure could possibly be changed in the most effective and efficient manner. There is much that is going on today that is called "diversion" from the juvenile justice system that is little more than referral upon referral to services for youths who would have not penetrated the system at all. This "widening of the net" is costly and has not resulted in a substantial reduction in cases processed by the juvenile courts.

There are too many "rip-offs" of precious and scarce tax dollars by ill-prepared and often unscrupulous community groups who are hopping on a new bandwagon. The importance of involving the community is paramount and apparent; the necessity of building in administrative controls and accountability are equally required to avoid the chaos of diverting funds from youth services rather than diverting youngsters from the juvenile justice system.

62

PRIVATE AND PUBLIC AGENCY INTEGRATION

Another important issue in this regard is the willingness of the private sector to handle those youngsters who are now enmeshed in juvenile correction programs. Over the years, many states have wisely encouraged private agency participation in the area of juvenile-delinquency prevention and juvenile rehabilitation work. The records of these private agencies have been mixed. Many have followed old-fashioned, traditional casework approaches with remnants of Lady Bountiful administrative concepts. They did serve a purpose with the more amenable, passive, and accidentally delinquent type of youngster. To think that these groups are willing or capable of handling all the youths now in training schools is an assumption that is not supported by experience or evidence. In one state, for example, a study indicated that private agencies consistently discriminated in their intake processes against delinquent and minority-group youths in favor of PINS and middle-class youngsters. While the private agencies were more than willing to have their operations principally supported by tax dollars, they consistently resisted state and municipal pressure to broaden their intake policies to serve more difficult youths. In some ways, it is difficult to fault them because of the lack of coordinated intake policy within most states and because they were subject to considerable pressure from private lay boards who were attuned to success stories about case outcome. Nevertheless, the almost total reliance upon the private sector to incorporate difficult delinquent youths into their programs must be considered carefully. Some of the worst child-care practices to be found are covered up in private childrens' institutions. While there is a dynamic and attractive quality in closing public institutions quickly in order to utilize the crisis situation to gain support and interest of the private sector, it is equally important to recognize that the private sector's record in handling difficult delinquent youths has not been noteworthy. Each state's public institutions

63

must be examined carefully to see how far they have departed from practical, decent child-care approaches. It is hypothesized here that the great majority of the states' training schools are more irrelevant than brutal and are more psychologically damaging than physically harmful.

The training schools today, with their congregate numbers, impersonal handling of children, operations run more for staff convenience than for meeting children's needs, overspecialized staff roles which segment rather than focus upon children, removal from the very pressure and problems with which children must learn to cope, are certainly not the answers in the field of juvenile correction. But there will always be some delinquent youngsters who need to have a moratorium from urban pressures, temptations, and problems.

We have always overestimated this number as we rationalized the need for large training schools and did not exhibit the political fortitude to move toward the community with our delinquency-intervention efforts.

Small (probably not more than a hundred beds—preferably on a coed basis) training schools should be part of any state's system in juvenile correction. The key to a juvenile correction system is diversification and not thinking that all problems can be handled in the community. We do not know enough about typology or human dynamics to be able to predict with confidence or accuracy what type of intervention works with what type youth. Certainly, the work of Grant, Warren, Schragg, Jesness, Moos, and others hold promise in the field of typology and its impact upon different types of programs for delinquents. We have much still to learn in this area. The tragedy has been that we have not built a continuum of services among all diverse components of a balanced juvenile correction program. The training school operates in isolation from the halfway house, which in turn is administratively and conceptually separate from the field aftercare workers, and are in turn separate from community forces, who are further removed from the intake processes of the agency which could let the community know what the agency really can offer its troubled youngsters.

The equivalent of a correctional barium test must be implemented to pull these seemingly coordinated yet functioningly disparate units together in a planning, orientation, and information-sharing series of experiences.

Furthermore, recognizing that the stage agency cannot hope to offer in the most efficient fashion all the services which delinquent youth require, the state must assume the role of standard setter, broker, monitor, and evaluator of the other players in the delinquency game. If the state wishes to subcontract group homes or other community approaches to the private sector, firm contracts spelling out precisely the fact that the state will be intensively involved in the intake decisions as to who will go to these private agencies is vital. Should a state wish to follow the lead of California and Washington in providing probation subsidies to localities to divert youths from the states' institutions, it is important to build in an evaluative component to insure that simply more of the old procedures which didn't work with youths in the past are not being advocated or implemented now.

THE RIGHTS OF YOUTH

The future will bring increasing challenges to the juvenile correctional system which are well warranted and long overdue. However, they pose dilemmas as well. Because of the lack of confidence in what the system has to offer, many more impediments are being placed in the path that leads to institutionalization. Legal counsel in the courts, ombudsmen in institutions, representation during parole-revocation hearings, restrictions on room confinement, punishment, mail censorship, length of incarceration, and a host of other areas are being probed and formalized through the courts in order to challenge the past arbitrary actions on the part of juvenile correctional administrators. Although these developments often frustrate the administrator and make his work more difficult, the enlightened administrator welcomes these checks and balances, which might well lead to a new perception on the part of young people that they are being treated impartially and fairly.

The courts, through their intervention, are increasingly raising questions about the effectiveness of treatment services offered. It will take close cooperation between the behavioral scientist and the lawyer to evolve a viable and practical set of standards as to what effective treatment really is. This area of legal challenge to the juvenile correctional process cannot be resolved through mere quantification of the numbers of psychiatrists, teachers, counseling sessions, recreation programs, and so on, which any correctional institution offers. The dilemma posed is how to measure the quality of the services so that it can be determined if youths are merely being incarcerated or helped, and if staff are merely being paid or are also working.

The future and nature of incarceration should be based upon the premise that the courts will move toward this disposition only if it can prove that youths cannot be handled in any other fashion.

Day-care centers, differentiated use of probation case loads, increased utilization of community volunteers in local programs, better liaison between field staff and schools, along with other approaches, should diminish the flow of cases to institutions. If incarceration is deemed necessary, the nature of the institutional offerings will be altered. The popular notion is that the institutional population which sifts through and fails in the community-based approach will be of such a hard-core nature that they will require the equivalent of locked, maximum-security units. This is not necessarily so, although it will be applicable for a few. As institutions become smaller, staff contacts and relationships can be substituted for steel, especially among younger offenders. In the past, the tragedy has been that many youths have deteriorated or did not adjust in large training-school operations, and juvenile correctional administrators have taken this to mean that they require a more secure and more controlled environment at the outset. What really occurred was that these youths became worse in our care.

Thus, even in the remaining institutions, the orientation in the main should be outward toward the public rather than inward toward the campus. As institutions become smaller in size, vacant buildings and cottages can be utilized to enrich the program offerings through such approaches as making them available as volunteer headquarters, weekend and overnight accommodations for parents who must travel and cannot afford lodging, settings for marathon sessions for aftercare workers who invite small groups of their case loads and families back up from the city to stabilize them rather than to reincarcerate them, staff training centers, quarters for minority-group staffs who might be willing to work three or four long days each week to put in their required hours but who would be reluctant to spend an entire workweek at a facility removed from an urban setting.

The emphasis on treatment will be the desire to allow young people to make as many meaningful decisions as possible about the nature of the institutional operation and the program there, as long as these decisions are not destructive to themselves or to others. In order to build toward maturity and decision-making, we must allow young people to have realistic alternatives in connection with program choices. To do otherwise would be to continue their infantilization. We must cut to the bare bone the ritualistic practices at play in the field which make for busywork on the part of scarce treatment people so that they can feel self-assured that they have thick diagnostic folders in case their decisions are questioned.

Elaborate, centralized, diagnostic facilities that test and assess young people in artificial settings should give way to decentralized units that can observe youngsters functioning under the very pressures with which they must learn to cope. Unilateral decision-making on the part of staff as to the readiness of youths for all aspects of their program including discharge must give way to intensive involvement on the part of the youths' peers to help make these decisions as well. School administrators, judges, business leaders, and mental health officials whose determinations and functioning clearly affect the juvenile correctional system must be encouraged, and in some areas legislatively mandated, to visit and become knowledgeable about the juvenile system's operations.

As we move toward the community towards public and private cooperation in providing youth services, it is incumbent upon all concerned to recognize that there is no single approach or easy panacea to solve the problems of juvenile delinquency which rise out of the loins of our societal mistakes, misunderstandings, and mismanagement.

5

As The Pendulum Swings
in England and Wales

Peter Marshall

JUVENILE JUSTICE IN ENGLAND AND WALES

The contemporary framework of juvenile justice in England and Wales may be seen as part of a continuing process which began in 1847. In that year justices were empowered to deal summarily with children under fourteen who had been charged with simple larceny, instead of committing them for trial to quarter sessions. Later, during the same century, summary trial was extended to embrace most cases against children. However, it was not until 1908 that separate courts were established for juveniles to remove them from the contaminating influence of "hardened criminals." The Children Act of that year made it obligatory for cases against children under 16 to be heard in a separate place or at a different time from adult courts. The concept of juvenile justice was given further definition by the Children and Young Persons Acts of 1933 and 1963, and it reached full contemporary flower, at least in concept, in the Children and Young Persons Act of 1969.

"CHILDREN IN TROUBLE"

Response to the 1969 Act has been heated and emotive; police, magistrates, parliamentarians, lawyers, journalists, and public alike have criticized the act and its effects to the point where it may be considered one of the most controversial pieces of criminal legislation of the decade. Clearly, then, it deserves some examination. Did the act indicate a completely new direction for juvenile justice, and was it based on new and radical concepts? The answer to both questions must be a qualified negative. The act was based largely on a government white paper, "Children in Trouble" (HMSO Cmnd. 3601), issued in 1968, and the views in that paper can be seen as a logical extension of the underlying philosophy of the Children Act of 1908. Its spirit may be discerned in the following quotation:

> "Juvenile delinquency has no single cause, manifestation or cure. Its origins are many, and the range of behaviour which it covers is equally wide. At some points it merges almost imperceptibly with behaviour which does not contravene the law. A child's behaviour is influenced by genetic, emotional and intellectual factors, his maturity, and his family, school, neighbourhood and wider social setting. It is probably a minority of children who grow up without misbehaving in ways which may be contrary to law. Frequently such behaviour is no more than an incident in the pattern of a child's normal development. But sometimes it is a response to unsatisfactory family or social circumstances, a result of boredom in and out of school, an indication of maladjustment or immaturity, or a symptom of a deviant, damaged or abnormal personality. Early recognition and full assessment are particularly important in these more serious cases. Variety and flexibility in the measures that can be taken are equally important if society is to deal effectively and appropriately with these manifold aspects of delinquency. These measures include supervision and support of the child in the family: the further development of the services working in the community and a variety of facilities for short-term and long-term care,

treatment and control, including some which are highly specialised.

The social consequences of juvenile delinquency range from minor nuisance to considerable damage and suffering for the community. An important object of the criminal law is to protect society against such consequences, but the community also recognises the importance of caring for those who are too young to protect themselves. Over recent years these two quite distinct grounds for action by society in relation to young people have been moving steadily closer together. It has become increasingly clear that social control of harmful behaviour by the young, and social measures to help and protect the young, are not distinct and separate processes. The aims of protecting society from juvenile delinquency, and of helping children in trouble to grow up into mature and law-abiding persons, are complementary and not contradictory.''

The 1969 Act embraced the philosophy of ''Children in Trouble'' and embodied many of the legislative recommendations made in the paper; but it was designed to be implemented in phases at the discretion of the secretary of state. Its most radical specific provisions, to   prohibit criminal proceedings for offenses other than homicide by children under the age of fourteen, (section 4) and the restriction of criminal proceedings for offenses by young persons over the age of fourteen but under seventeen (section 5), have yet to be implemented.

Section 5 would require prosecutions to be brought only by a ''qualified informant''—a servant of the Crown, a police officer, or a member of a local government authority and the qualified informant would have a statutory duty to determine that no other method of dealing with the case would be adequate before he laid an information before a court; additionally, he must have informed the appropriate local authority of his intentions and have sought their observations.

In brief, the intentions of the white paper and the act may be summarized thus: criminal prosecutions other than for homicide would no longer be brought against those under fourteen; criminal offenses committed by youths under fourteen could provide grounds for taking care proceedings, but it would be necessary to provide that the child was in need of care and control which he or she would be unlikely to receive unless the court made an order; criminal charges against those over fourteen would no longer be brought unless the prosecutor considered noncriminal response inappropriate, had sought the views of a statutory welfare agency, and could satisfy a court that a prosecution was necessary. These provisions indicate the clear intention that greater consideration should be given to informal nonjudicial disposals, that greater consultation should take place between relevant agencies, and that court proceedings should be viewed as a last resort.

Underlining this emphasis on a social welfare response to juvenile offenders and those at risk was the reorganization of social services following the Report of the Interdepartmental Committee on local authority social services—the Seebohm Report—to coordinate the necessary resources and skills needed to implement programs for juveniles as well as for other needy sections of the community.

PRESENT DECISIONS

Unlike Scotland, there is no general system of public prosecutors in England and Wales. With the exception of certain cases which must be reported to the director of public prosecutions and other offenses which require the attorney general's fiat, police discretion to prosecute remains unfettered in general law. Section 5 of the 1969 Act, if implemented, would circumscribe that discretion, but there is no indication that it is likely to be implemented in the near future, and precourt decision-making must be seen in that light. (Some restraint is also imposed by the presumption of *doli incapax*, which presumes that a person over the age of ten, but under fourteen has not reached the age of discretion, but this is rebuttable by strong evidence of a mischievous disposition.)

The police are the principal agency likely to become aware that a child or young person has committed a criminal offense. If the child is under the age of ten, criminal proceedings cannot be brought, although police may initiate care proceedings if other evidence is available to show the child is in need of care or control. Between the ages of ten and fourteen, criminal proceedings may be brought if there is evidence to rebut *doli incapax*, and between the ages of fourteen and sixteen there are no specific legal restraints in force which inhibit criminal proceedings.

Most police forces in England and Wales have some form of procedure to process juvenile offenders separately from adult offenders. The two main branches of development have been the juvenile liaison scheme and the juvenile bureau.

JUVENILE LIAISON

Juvenile liaison originated in Liverpool in 1949 in an attempt to prevent juvenile crime. Selected officers were instructed to take such measures as were practicable and desirable to achieve that end. Essentially the scheme was concerned with predelinquency, but it involved a system of selective cautioning of identified offenders and postcautioning supervision and counseling by police liaison officers.

The initial instructions of the chief constable,[1] exhorted police to:

---

1.   *Juvenile Liaison Officers*—A New Police Approach to the Prevention of Juvenile Crime. Published by Liverpool City Police, 1954.

(i) invoke the assistance of all those interested in the welfare of young children to prevent juvenile offenders from committing further offences.

(ii) as the most important people in this respect are the parents of the children concerned, to visit them and secure their co-operation in ways and means of guiding the child's future behaviour.

(iii) establish liaison with head teachers, ministers of religion, youth club leaders and other persons in close contact with children, or who are especially affected by delinquency, so that early notice of delinquent tendencies can be obtained.

(iv) co-operate with probation officers and other professional welfare workers without usurping any of their functions.

(v) keep records and statistics containing relevant information about juvenile offenders coming to notice.

(vi) maintain regular contact with juveniles who have been cautioned by the police or referred to juvenile liaison officers for attention.

(vii) introduce juveniles into youth clubs and encourage their continued attendance.

(viii) attend committee meetings sponsored by the Central Juvenile Delinquency Committee.

(ix) arrange monthly conferences of juvenile liaison officers under the chairmanship of the Chief Inspector in charge of the Scheme for the interchange of ideas and experience and the discussion of problems and difficulties.

These pioneering instructions provide the genesis for much police activity today in the field of juvenile delinquency.

JUVENILE BUREAUS

General and marked increases in recorded crime and growing demands made on limited resources across the whole range of police activity have placed severe limits on the extent to which police can engage in predelinquency supervision. Consequently, greater emphasis has been placed on developing a structured capacity to process identified delinquents in a constructive way which will be in tune with wider developments in juvenile justice. Systems developed from this basis are generally called juvenile bureau schemes, and the Metropolitan Police Scheme is one of the most comprehensive of its kind.

By April 1969 all divisions of the Metropolitan Police in London were operating juvenile bureaus in anticipation of the Children and Young Persons Act of 1969, which was implemented in 1971 (with the exception of those major provisions already referred to). In London, prior to 1969 it was the practice to deal with juvenile offenders very much in the same way as adults. If after preliminary investigation at the police station credible evidence to support the arrest was available, the offender was charged and brought before a court. With the establishment of juvenile bureaus, a more comprehensive basis for the exercise of discretion was created involving consultation with other concerned agencies.

The procedure well warrants closer examination. When a juvenile is arrested he is taken to the police station and the offense is investigated to establish the credibility of the arrest and the existence of sufficient evidence to place before a court should proceedings subsequently be deemed appropriate. The juvenile's parents or guardians will be invited to attend the station, and after procedures have been explained to them the juvenile will be released to their custody. An important step at this stage is the provision to the parents of a written explanation of bureau procedure on a form which also invites them to seek legal advice.

In certain circumstances the juvenile will not be released from custody; for example, when the offense is a particularly serious one, when his background or circumstances precludes the granting of bail, or when parents or guardians refuse to accept responsibility for his custody. In such cases he would be charged with the offense and appear in court in due course. (Currently less than 20 percent of all juveniles arrested in the Metropolitan Police District are charged forthwith; this procedure being reserved in the main for serious recidivist offenders, for those accused of grave crimes, and for those whose release might defeat the ends of justice or be contrary to their own interests.)

In those cases where a charge is not preferred, case papers are sent to the juvenile bureau, together with a certificate from the private complainant (if there is one) to the effect that he or she is willing to leave the question of disposal with the police. If the complainant refuses such a certificate and a prima facie case is made out, court proceedings will invariably ensue.

A typical London bureau will be staffed by a superintendent or chief inspector, (who is also the divisional community liaison officer), one inspector and one sergeant, and some six constables. Its main function will be to gather information—from social services departments, educational welfare officers, probation service, police records, and home visits—to insure that an informed decision on the disposition of the case can be taken by the bureau chief. Home visits, involving interviews with parents and their children in the domestic setting, usually provide valuable insight into parental attitudes and give some pointers to the degree of family support likely to be available in the event of a noncourt disposition.

When bureau inquiries are completed, the officer in charge will have all the evidence necessary to present the case at court, together with a comprehensive report on the child's background and an awareness of any other agency's interest. Communication between police and social services agencies is clearly vital to obviate duality of action and to insure that police are fully aware of background circumstances.

Dispositions open to the bureau chief are: prosecution; caution; no further action; or, in rare cases, care proceedings. In many cases, the decision will be straightforward; a stable home background in combination with no previous record of delinquency and supportive parents will usually indicate that a caution would be the most appropriate disposal. An unstable background combined with a poor delinquency record and negative parental attitudes will predispose toward a court appearance. In a relatively small number of cases, a difficult and delicate choice will be involved, but it should be clearly understood that previous offenses will not automatically lead to a court disposition any more than their absence will automatically lead to a caution.

POLICE CAUTIONS

Cautions are administered in the presence of parents by a uniformed police officer not below the rank of chief inspector. They are recorded, and particulars are supplied to statutory social services; they may also be referred to in any subsequent juvenile court proceedings. Before a case can be disposed of by caution, the juvenile must admit the offense, parents must agree to the procedure, and complainants must accept the police decision.

Separate dispositions may be made in respect of joint offenders.

JUVENILE BUREAU STAFF

Appointments to bureaus are not made on a permanent basis; an optimum length of service for a member would be about four years. Some formal training is given, but emphasis is placed on the selection of officers from the general-duty field who have a good background of practical police experience together with an interest in, and understanding of, the types of problems with which they are likely to deal. Maturity of outlook, sincerity, and open-mindedness are the principal characteristics sought.

Early criticism of the scheme included that police lacked formal training and professional social work qualifications. However, it was soon recognized that the police role had always embodied a significant "social work" content, and the anticipated rift between the professional social worker and the "horny-handed cop" never developed to any great extent.

The issue of training is constantly under review, and some seven years of operational experience have provided opportunities for in-service training to supplement the abundance of common sense acquired from general police experience of dealing with people, a quality often lacking in some inexperienced, though professionally qualified social workers.

Bureaus have developed an important secondary role over the years—involvement in schools. Each bureau has a coordinating role for its division's police schools program. Informal visits to infants schools by the local bobby on the beat; formal involvement of police in senior schools' projects; film shows, lectures; discussions; competitions; and even, in one instance, police taking over the syllabus of a comprehensive school and providing all the teaching resources for a one-day session on social studies indicate the importance placed upon police-pupil contacts in a constructive setting. The community liaison responsibilities of the head of a bureau provide an even wider setting for the development of an effective relationship between police, youth, and other agencies in the field. Despite the growing demands made on limited police resources, this investment in youth is seen as a major priority.

JUVENILE COURTS

Special juvenile courts were established in England and Wales in 1908. Since then, growing emphasis has been placed on the welfare of the child, specifically within the framework of the criminal law with its traditional regard for procedures designed to protect the interests of the individual as well as those of society.

Generally, juveniles benches are made up of lay justices appointed by the Lord Chancellor from local nominations, and in the inner London area members are required to have some knowledged expertise or interest in the problems of children and young persons. Occasionally stipendiary magistrates from adult courts will sit in juvenile courts in the inner London area.

Particular emphasis is placed on separating juveniles from adult offenders, and juvenile courts may not be held in places where an adult court has sat within one hour before or will sit within one hour after the juvenile hearing.

A child or young person charged with an offense other than homicide must be tried summarily unless he is charged jointly with a person over 17, and the court considers it in the interests of justice that both should be committed for trial, or unless he is a young person over the age of 14 and the offense is punishable in the case of an adult by imprisonment for 14 years or more and the court considers that if found guilty he should be detained for a period not exceeding the maximum term for which an adult would be liable.

Rules and procedures are designed to reduce formality and insure simplicity; the charge must be explained to the defendant in simple language; parents are allowed to participate in the defense and cross-examine witnesses; and the court will assist an unaided juvenile where he makes assertions instead of cross- examining witnesses. Parents must be allowed to make statements or representations to the court, and extraneous background reports must be taken into account.

DECISIONS OF THE COURT

Bearing in mind the paramountcy placed upon the interests

and welfare of the defendant, juvenile courts, following a finding of guilt, have the following range of options open to them:

ABSOLUTE OR CONDITIONAL DISCHARGE
As with an adult court.

FINES
A fine may be imposed for any indictable offense which is tried summarily and for any other offense for which an adult could be fined. A fine on a young person (over fourteen but under seventeen) may not exceed £50, and for a child (over ten but under fourteen) may not exceed £10. The court has power to order the parent or guardian to pay the fine and, in the case of a child, must so order unless satisfied that the parents have not contributed to the commission of the offense by neglecting to exercise care or control.

BINDING OVER
The court has power to order a parent or guardian to enter into a recognizance to take proper care of, and exercise proper control over, a child or young person. The recognizance should not exceed £50, and may be imposed for up to three years or until the juvenile reaches the age of eighteen, whichever is the shorter.

SUPERVISION ORDER
A juvenile may be placed by order of the court under the supervision of the local authority social services department or, in the case of an offender who has attained the age of twelve, under the supervision of the probation service. Orders may contain specific requirements as to residence or medical treatment, and their object is to provide continuing and flexible social welfare support within the context of a court adjudication. As with a binding over, a supervision order may be imposed for up to three years or until the youth's eighteenth birthday.

CARE ORDER

On conviction for an offense which in the case of an adult would be punishable by imprisonment, a juvenile may be committed to the care of a local authority. A care order made before a juvenile reaches the age of sixteen remains in force until his eighteenth birthday is reached; one made after the age of sixteen remains in force until the age of nineteen, although orders may be discharged by a court at any time.

Supervision orders and care orders may be imposed as a result of care proceedings as well as of criminal proceedings.

ATTENDANCE CENTER ORDER

For those juveniles perceived as not yet committed to a criminal career but nevertheless found guilty of an offense punishable in the case of an adult by imprisonment, the court may make an attendance center order to impose punishment through loss of leisure. Attendance centers usually exist in large urban areas and in the main are run by volunteer policemen or teachers. The number of hours of attendance ordered by the court may not be less than twelve unless the juvenile is under the age of fourteen or more than twenty-four. Attendance sessions are usually for periods of not less than two hours on alternate Saturdays (perhaps those Saturdays when the favorite soccer team is playing "at home") until the order is discharged. The regime, imposed at the discretion of the person in charge, will contain some elements of discipline and may embrace some form of handicrafts or physical activity, but the aim is to "warn off" the social nuisance by a minimal and fleeting punishment.

The 1969 Act empowers the secretary of state to withdraw detention-center facilities, but at the time of writing there is no indication that he is likely to exercise this power in the immediate future.

DETENTION-CENTER ORDER

Juvenile detention centers are perceived as providing a more severe treatment regime for fourteen- to seventeen-year-olds found guilty of an offense for which an adult might be imprisoned. They offer a disciplined framework within which full-time education facilities are available for inmates of school age, together with work schemes covering a wide range of activities. They are designed to provide a short-term form of treatment characterized by firmness and discipline. Orders are normally for a period of three months and are subject to remission for good behavior and the provision of twelve months of aftercare.

BORSTAL

Juvenile courts may commit a young offender of fifteen or over to the Crown Court with a recommendation for confinement in a borstal if he is found guilty of an offense for which an adult would be liable to imprisonment. The sentence is indeterminate and ranges between six months and two years and, although primarily custodial, places emphasis on training, education, and leadership. There is a statutory requirement of two years' postborstal supervision which is normally carried out by the probation service.

GRAVE CRIMES

For certain grave crimes, courts may impose an indeterminate sentence of detention. In the case of homicide, the sentence will be detention "during Her Majesty's Pleasure," and for other crimes for which an adult might be sentenced to fourteen years' imprisonment or more the sentence may be for any period not exceeding the maximum for adults. Detention thus imposed is served in accordance with directions given by the secretary of state, who may direct that the juvenile be detained in a community home until reaching the age of nineteen.

DEFERRED SENTENCES

A Juvenile court may, on a finding of guilt, defer disposition for not more than six months in order that consideration might be given to the juvenile's subsequent conduct and any change in his circumstances.

COMPENSATION

A compensation order may be made in addition to any other order, up to a maximum of £400. Such an order is entirely within the discretion of the juvenile court and is not dependent upon application by the victim: it is designed to take into account personal injury, loss, or damage resulting from any offenses for which there is a finding of guilt or which has been taken into consideration by the court.

POST-TRIAL DECISION MAKING

We have seen that one of the major effects of the 1969 Act was to remove from the court much of the power to make specific dispositions regarding the subsequent treatment of juvenile offenders and to give greater discretion to social service departments. A supervision order may require the supervised person to comply with certain directions of the supervisor as to residence, reporting, and participation in certain activities, but it is within the discretion of the supervisor to determine the extent to which he will exercise any of the powers conferred on him by the court order.

"Children in Trouble" pointed out that existing powers of courts distinguished sharply between those which involved complete removal from the home and those which did not. It urged the creation of some form of "intermediate treatment" which would allow the child to remain in his own home but would also bring him into contact with a different environment. The 1969 Act, in its provisions for supervision, acknowledged this need and provided the framework of direction at the discretion of the supervisor within which intermediate-treatment schemes could be established. Regional planning committees are empowered to devise local schemes within the framework of supervision orders and are required to submit their proposals for the approval of the secretary of state.

Intermediate treatment schemes embrace both residential and nonresidential facilities and are devoid of any element of judicial punishment. The facilities they provide are intended for young people generally and not solely for those who have been dealt with by a juvenile court. Government approval has been given to schemes submitted by all regions of England and Wales, but their viability and effectiveness is more apparent in intention than execution, and this is particularly tragic, since their concept represented a major part of the new approach advocated by "Children in Trouble" and incorporated in the 1969 Act.

Supervision orders are largely carried out by social workers employed by local-authority social services departments, who are enjoined "to advise, assist and befriend" the juvenile. In the large urban centers, lack of resources, excessive case loads, and the lack of effective intermediate-treatment schemes, have meant that token supervision is often a reality, and many youngsters continue their criminal activities without any real restraint or effective support.

If effective decision-making in the area of supervision is partially rendered impotent by lack of resources and coordinated drive, what of the other major innovation, the care order? Here again, wide discretion is placed in the hands of the local authority to determine how they will exercise their responsibilities for care. The act implies that at least part of the period of care should involve removal from home environment, placing the juvenile with foster parents, in a community home, a voluntary home, or under such other arrangements as seem appropriate.

A local authority in whose care a juvenile has been placed may make use of an assessment center where psychiatric, medical, and other reports may be prepared to help arrive at the most appropriate form of treatment. Again, particularly in urban areas, resources are limited and many youngsters made the subject of care orders may not be sent to assessment centres.

Community homes range in concept from the therapeutic-treatment center to the disciplined framework of the old approved school, but, catering as they do to the deprived as well as to the delinquent, they cannot meet all the demands that are made on them; and, crucially, they can be selective in the intake to the point that a juvenile thought suitable for a particular community home may be refused a place there by the staff because he is considered disruptive. This discretion, combined with the general lack of secure accommodation, means that many of the most criminally active youngsters cannot be contained in a controlled environment until they qualify for confinement in a borstal, and in the intervening period they are unresponsive to supervision in the community.

CONCLUSION

Although there can be little dispute that the 1969 Act has failed to contain significant increases in recorded juvenile crime, its aims and intentions are still the subject of passionate debate. Few would disregard the argument that the resources envisaged in the White Paper and the Act itself have not been provided in sufficient measure, but many would argue that the lumping together of the deprived and the depraved provides a system where neither group receives effective support and that the resources available for the treatment of the deprived are vitiated. Public debate will continue and emotion will play its part, but concepts such as "the child's right to punishment" and "society's right to post signposts and protect itself" will be heard more and more as the argument goes on.

6

The Scottish Rejection of the Juvenile Courts

Beti Jones and G. J. Murray

INTRODUCTION

This chapter describes the children's panel system in Scotland which was introduced in 1971 to replace the previous juvenile courts. For comparative purposes, it is in three parts— prehearing, hearing, and posthearing—to parallel the specification of pretrial, trial, and posttrial. The Introduction and Part I explain that the system was the result of much discussion during the 1960s and earlier. It is the most significant shift of juvenile justice in Scotland, removing children in all but the most serious cases from the courts to a children's hearing, a lay tribunal openly recruited and concerned statutorily only with the interests of the child. Compulsory measures of care must be considered necessary before a child appears at a hearing. This has meant that the police now play an even larger part in diversion by means of police warnings. A new official has been introduced, called the reporter, to whom children offending or offended against are reported; and the compulsory-care criterion means that in many cases the reporter, after assessing information about a child, does not bring him before a hearing.

Part II outlines the open recruitment, the selection, and the composition of the children's panels from whom the members of a hearing of three are drawn. It emphasizes the realized aim of selecting persons with capacity for, interest in, and experience with, children; of a wide (and frequently youthful) age range; and with a balance of the sexes; and also the efforts still being made to achieve a closer correlation to the social structure of each area than it has been possible so far to achieve. The hearing cannot exercise its jurisdiction unless the facts are accepted or established by the sheriff court. The procedure is private (the press may be present but cannot publish names). It is informal and depends on the participation of the parents. Its disposals are basically supervision, either at home with suitable treatment programs if available, or in a residential establishment. Its disposals may be appealed to the sheriff court but seldom are.

Part III discusses the residential and supervisory resources available, together with the developing intermediate-treatment programs. It points out the difficulties that can arise from the long lead time necessary between the statutory recognition of a new concept and the provision of the necessary treatment and staff resources on the ground. The regular reviewing of cases at not more than annual intervals by hearings with consequential changes in disposals are put forward as one of the system's main strengths. The paper concludes with a general assessment of the system.

HISTORICAL BACKGROUND

THE JUVENILE COURT

The children's hearing system requires to be explained in the light of the juvenile court it has largely (but not quite entirely) replaced. The juvenile courts were set up in 1908 and were a very considerable step forward. They recognized that children should be treated separately from adults; that the arrangements for children in the fairly typical sheriff, burgh, and justice-of-the-peace (JP) court should differ from those for adults; and that there was a need to have regard to the child's welfare and to secure measures of education and training in his best interests. Subsequently, Scottish legislation in the 1930s recommended a specific transfer of jurisdiction for children and young offenders to specially constituted JP juvenile courts, with specially suitable justices. But only four out of over thirty Scottish authorities introduced these arrangements. There remained implicit in the system the difficulty that the juvenile courts were still basically the same as the adult courts, with modified disposals. The sheriff, bailies, or justices of the peace[1] in the sheriff, burgh (town), and JP (county) courts were concerned with the establishment of guilt or innocence in the formal court setting. They had to deal with the appropriate sentence and somehow fit into this the welfare of the child. This might well demand a course of action seen as too severe (or too trivial) for the normal considerations governing sentence.

POST-WAR REFORMS

While the juvenile courts were grappling with these problems, the very unsatisfactory and complex arrangement for dealing with children in public care under a variety of local authority committees led to the setting up of the Curtis Committee in England, and the Clyde Committee in Scotland. These resulted in the Children Act 1948, which produced local authority children's departments in Great Britain with an obligation to consider the needs and abilities of the children in their care. The growth of a specialized child-care service was followed by an in-

----

1. The sheriff is a qualified lawyer in a full-time judicial post. Bailies and justices of the peace are lay magistrates. Burgh and JP courts have just been replaced by district courts with either stipendiary (ie., full-time lawyers) or lay magistrates.

creasing realization that frequently more preventive action was needed in relation to the whole family situation if children were able to remain with their family. The work of the Ingleby and McBoyle committees was followed by the Children Act 1963, which enabled positive help to be given to families. The Ingleby Committee in England and Wales also suggested further modifications of the juvenile court system. A subsequent ambitious white paper, "The Child, the Family and the Offender", proposed "family courts" for England and Wales. But in the event, following a modified white paper, "Children in Trouble", England and Wales got the Children and Young Persons Act of 1969. This introduced only modifications, although substantial ones, to the juvenile court system.

The Scottish juvenile courts obviously had to come under scrutiny too; and in 1962 the Kilbrandon Committee on Children and Young Persons was set up. It reported in 1964. Its analysis was that children appearing before the courts, whether for offenses or as being in need of care and protection showed a basic similarity in a failure of the upbringing process and had a common need for special measures of education and training. These would involve working closely with the parents and required the formation in each area of a locally based treatment authority. The existing juvenile court arrangements did not make this easy; a court system, with its emphasis, however muted, on decisions on guilt or innocence and punishment of the guilty, was inappropriate. The committee was clear that there must be a separation of the fact-finding part of the process from the consideration of treatment and that this could hardly be done under the existing system.

The committee's solution was to take juveniles under sixteen out of the criminal system except for the gravest cases; to replace the juvenile courts by juvenile panels; to have cases sifted out and referred to the panel only by an official called the reporter; and to set up a new statutory social-education department in education-authority areas as a matching fieldwork agency to provide some background reports and recommendations for treatment measures. The panels could act only when the facts were admitted. Disputed grounds would be determined by the sheriff (i.e., by a legally qualified member of the judiciary in a court), as would appeals against panel decision.

Subsequently the government, in a Scottish white paper, "Social Work and the Community", and subsequently in legislation, the Social Work (Scotland) Act 1968 (Part III), set out proposals reflecting closely the Kilbrandon Report's suggestions. The 1968 act was, however, largely devoted to the setting up of local authority social work departments to provide an integrated social work service, including a service to the new children's panels. The very comprehensive powers given to these new departments, including a general duty to promote social welfare, gave local authorities a wide positive role in meeting and indeed searching out needs, and in encouraging individuals, families, and groups to help solve problems with their own resources or with the aid of resources available within the community.

The date for the introduction of the new social work departments was fixed at 17 November 1969. The introduction of the new system of children's panels was left until later to allow the departments time to settle down and prepare for the new obligations that the provision of services for the children's panels would bring. It also allowed time for the setting up and training of the children's panels, the appointment of the appropriate officials, and the making of the necessary procedural regulations. The hope had been to introduce the system one year later. In fact, children's hearings began to operate on 15 April 1971. Children's panels operate in children's hearings of three panel members.

What are the key principles against which the practice of the children's hearing should be set? These have not been set out in much detail in the 1968 act, and the statutory bones have to be filled out from the Kilbrandon Report and the white paper of 1966.

First, children are to be dealt with outside the court system except for the most serious cases. The new children's hearing is not a court. If facts are disputed before the hearing, the case must go to the sheriff for establishment of the facts but thereafter returns to the hearing for disposal. The children's hearing is not, then, concerned with guilt or innocence but with the disposal of the child. In fixing this disposal, the hearing's only statutory obligation is to have regard to "the best interests of the child." There is nothing here of "deterrence" or "retribution," or of punishment except as a treatment.

Second, the child himself should not come before a hearing unless the referring agency or person and, more important, the reporter assessing the referral, consider that he is "in need of compulsory measures of care." Nor can the hearing prescribe any compulsory residential or nonresidential supervision unless that criterion is satisfied.

The question in both these cases is how far it is really practicable for the children's hearings not to consider the interests of the community as well as the interests of the child.

Third, particular store is set in the Kilbrandon Report and in the 1968 Act on the degree of assessment that may be possible in the reports prepared, particularly for the cases that go before a hearing. This reinforces the treatment aspect of the hearing's work. The question is the degree of sophistication in practice attainable in assessment at the present time.

Fourth, the informality of the hearings and the emphasis on dialogue is plainly designed to lead the hearing away from the adversary and advocacy situation that marks trials; to improve the quality of information and discussion and the solutions that are arrived at. The question is the extent to which normal legal safeguards were being maintained while not affecting the free exchange of information.

Fifth, a wide range of treatment resources must be available. The reader must reach his own verdict in the light of the following description of the procedures. It would not, however, be surprising if he reaches the same conclusion one research team did that the system is "an empirical amalgam of welfare, due process and control."

PART I

PRE-HEARING PROCEDURES[2]

A child under sixteen gets into the system if he is referred to the reporter by some person or agency which believes that he may be in need of compulsory measures of care. In 1974 there were over 31,000 referrals (6 per 1,000 population). A child is most likely to be referred to the reporter for having committed an offense or offenses (over 90 percent of cases). But another ground for referral is truancy or falling into bad associations. Or he may have been offended against or have been neglected. Referrals to the reporter may be made by the public, by the social work department, by the education authority, or by other agencies. But the bulk of referrals are made by the police. The fact that a child has committed an offense and this is known to the police does not necessarily mean that he will be referred to the reporter.

POLICE WARNINGS
If his offense is minor and/or he is a first offender, the police may decide to give him an informal warning, or a formal warning before a superintendent. These police warnings have increased substantially since the inception of the system, as many minor offenses are not considered to merit compulsory measures of

2. The flow chart at Annex A and the statistics at Annex B may be found useful for references when reading this section.

care. In 1974 there were over 10,000 (2 per 1,000 population) police warnings. A number of police authorities also issue warnings at the request of the reporter. There is no specific provision within the children's hearing arrangements for dealing with minor offenses that are not considered to be manifestations of difficulties requiring compulsory measures of care. The police role is therefore that much harder, in this area where old penalties are no longer available, and more substantial treatment is not necessary (or sometimes not quickly available). This question is returned to later in the conclusions.

CASES REFERRED TO THE PROCURATOR FISCAL

At the other end of the spectrum a variety of more serious cases also do not come within the scope of the children's hearing system at this stage. The 1968 Act did not restrict the power of the Lord Advocate (the government's chief law officer in Scotland, who has responsibility for the public prosecutors in Scotland, the procurators fiscal) to instruct the prosecution of children in the courts. There are standing arrangements under which certain kinds of offenses, for example, serious cases involving offenses against the person—forfeiture of weapons and, where technically necessary for proof (namely, some cases where the child is charged jointly with an adult), are scrutinized by the procurator fiscal in order to decide if prosecution is appropriate. When a prosecution is decided on, the reporter takes no further action. There has been a determined effort to reduce the number of these cases brought before the sheriff court. After increasing for years, these were reduced in 1974 by 10 percent (to under 3,000 a year), but this is still a substantial number. The court may, however, and in some cases must, remit the case to the children's hearing for advice; and may also remit the case for disposal.

WHAT THE REPORTER DOES

The reporter is the official with the main responsibility for organizing the mechanics of the system; but more important, he has the key decision-making function about whether or not to bring a child reported to him before a hearing. In this he has an absolute discretion analogous to that possessed in individual cases in Scotland by the procurator fiscal in relation to prosecutions. (Scotland has a public prosecution system with only limited rights of prosecution by private persons.) Reporters are appointed by the twelve regional or islands local authorities; but their operational independence, and the central government interest in their justice-related functions, is exemplified in the fact that without the consent of the secretary of state a reporter may not be removed from office by a local authority.

When the reporter receives a referral, he makes such initial investigations as he may think necessary. This may involve obtaining reports from the social work department, the school, the police, or other reporters and departments in other areas. The reporter then has three main courses he may follow:

(1) *He may decide no further action is required by the panel system.* This informal decision of "no further action" reflects the reporter's view that compulsory measures of care are not needed in relation to this referral. It might, however, cover a range of informal actions or have a variety of explanations. It may be clear from reports that the home is supportive and firm and that the offense will not be repeated; that reparation is being made; or that family difficulties have not been picked up by the social work department. Or, less cheerfully, the child may already be under supervision but the situation plainly does not merit residential supervision.

(2) *He may refer the case to the social work department with a view to their making voluntary arrangements for the advice, guidance, and assistance of the child and his family.* Sometimes he may consider it sufficient to have a voluntary arrangement with the family regarding a referral to the social work department. In effect, the help made available ought to be very similar to that provided under statutory supervision, and it would be only in cases where an element of compulsion was felt to be

necessary that the case would go before the hearing. In practice, the pressures on some social work departments are currently very great, and the use of voluntary arrangements would not seem to have been substantial in many areas; such arrangements would inevitably have to be given a lesser order of attention than the statutory supervision requirements made by a hearing.

(3) *He may bring the child before a children's hearing:* (i) if he is satisfied that there is evidence of at least one ground for referral; and (ii) if it appears to him that the child is in need of compulsory measures of *care.*

Over 15,000 cases were referred to children's hearings in 1974. If the reporter decides a child should be referred to a hearing, he will then arrange a children's hearing; obtain the necessary background reports provided by the social work department, school, and other agencies; and insure that the parents and the child are notified. The parents have a *duty* to attend unless excused, and they also have a *right* to attend.

Reporters as a whole normally bring about half of their referrals before hearings. In 1974 the figures were over 15,000 out of 31,000 (3 per 1,000 population). The difficult question is the extent to which questions of community interest in practice influence referrals. Does the fact that a child with several acts of very minor vandalism is more likely to come before a hearing than a child who has committed only one or two mean that the reporter considers that a pattern is beginning to emerge which makes compulsory care seem necessary? Or does it simply mean that the reporter recognizes that public attitudes require that some action be taken? It is plain, in any case, that the reporter is the most important diversionary element; and also, as it is not the usual practice for the reporter to see the child and the parents at the decision-making stage, it is clear that much must depend on the information the reporter gets.

Assessment of a child's needs is, of course, relevant at all stages of the process—before a child is referred to a hearing;

after a hearing has, in emergency cases, sent a child at once to a place of safety; or after a hearing has been adjourned for more information or is held for a later review. It is at the stage at which good information becomes available that it is possible to sift out the "no-action" cases. If a reporter can get thorough initial information, he can sift it himself. Otherwise, at the hearing stage the hearing sifts and engages in the diversionary process. Ideally, the material usually presented to the hearing would include lengthy school and social work background reports, with the crucial document being an assessment prepared by a multi-disciplinary assessment team, including social workers, educational psychologists, psychiatrists, and pediatricians. These would be prepared while the child was at home or in residential care for a short period. These teams do not exist everywhere, and currently the more usual situation is to have a school and social work department's background report available at the hearing. The reporter may sometimes depend on oral consultations and on his own assessment that, for example, general difficulties seem to be arising in a number of key areas, such as home, school, and neighborhood, and that referral to a hearing seems necessary. A social-background report is a statutory requirement for a hearing, and in practice school reports are always obtained. These reports must be made available to panel members three days before the hearing.

PART II

THE HEARING

INTRODUCTION

If there is one inappropriate word for a children's hearing, it is "trial." The hearing does not concern itself with the establishment of facts, which are either accepted immediately or have to be established elsewhere. It is perhaps best described as a private treatment discussion between the interested parties in which the three hearing members represent the community and have the ultimate decisionmaking power. This section will start, then, with a description of the panel members, how they are recruited, selected, and trained, and who are the other participants in the hearing.

Each hearing consists of three children's panel members chosen by the chairman of the panel or under standing arrangements; each sex must be represented. Members are drawn from the children's panel which the secretary of state is required to appoint for each regional and islands authority. There are currently over 1,600 panel members ranging from about 900 in Strathclyde to about 10 in Orkney. Many of the larger panels operate through a system of informal area panels. The aim is an approximate balance of the sexes, and the age range is from about twenty to a maximum of sixty.

Children's panels are recruited by open advertisement, and subsequent selection procedures, normally involving interviews and group discussion and sometimes discussions with specialist interviewers such as psychologists. The responsibility for obtaining and recommending possible members to the secretary of state rests with children's panel advisory committees in these authorities (with two members from the local authority, and three including the chairman, nominated by the secretary of state). Children's panel members undertake the specially organized preservice and in-service preparation run along nationally laid down guidelines. This includes lectures; videotapes; role playing; observation at hearings; meetings with social workers, police, and assessment center staff; and visits to establishments and local facilities.

The aim in recruiting panel members has been to recruit people with knowledge and experience in dealing with children and families, an interest in their needs, and the capacity to communicate. Good response to recruitment campaigns and careful selection has insured a large measure of success. Less fully successful has been the other main aim of drawing the members from a wide range of occupation, neighborhood, age groups, and income groups. The age grouping has been good, with a median age of early 40s, which is very young for major public service, and a considerable number of panel members in their 20s. It has proved more difficult to find panel members in the right proportions from all social classes, or in requisite numbers from areas producing many of the children with problems. But the situation is slowly improving, and even at present about one fifth of the panel members are manual workers. The children's panel members as a group have also become considerably involved in many areas in training new members, in planning resources, and in stimulating discussion about these new developments in the community. They have earned for themselves the description by a distinguished Scottish academic in a forthcoming article as "a remarkable example of creative voluntary activity."

Every effort is made to have the child and his parents at the hearing, ranging from holding hearings at various times of day and evening to ultimate and perhaps counterproductive sanctions of fining. These efforts have been largely successful. Parents have a duty to attend, and their attendance is crucial to the participative concept of the hearing. They also have a right to attend all parts of the hearing. The hearing may exclude the child when it feels this is appropriate.

The reporter has prepared the papers concerned with the grounds for referral and may be involved in explaining them or in explaining his reasons for considering that these grounds justified a referral to the hearing; and generally, he is concerned with guiding the hearing on its procedure. But the reporter's role is less fundamental in the hearing situation than in the preliminary decision-making.

The social worker has perhaps the key official role. As far as possible the social worker present is the social worker who will have visited the family prior to the hearing (or indeed know the family already) and will have prepared the social-background report which is the hearing's principal source of information.

The social worker will also be conversant with the treatment possibilities, and may well have a specific recommendation to the hearing.

Legal aid is not available at hearings, but the parents and/or the child may have a representative or a friend at the hearing; including a legal representative. Developing interest in child representation in various types of adoption and custody proceedings has extended to child-protection cases; for example, where in extreme cases there are finely balanced arguments about the advisability of giving back to his parents at their request a young child when the child has been placed formally under the supervision of the local authority. The Children Act of 1975 now requires a chairman of a hearing to consider whether a child requires a separate representative and, if so, to appoint one for him. (This provision has not yet been implemented.)

Apart from the six or seven persons mentioned above, the hearings are private, and no members of the public are admitted. The press have been given by Parliament the right to attend, which is only occasionally exercised. Other observers such as trainee panel members and researchers may be admitted by the chairman, and usually no more than two are admitted.

The setting is regarded as very important to the promotion of discussion and presents a contrast tó the different-level, very structured court setting. Hearings usually take place in an ordinary, not-too-large room with a central table around which sit the persons concerned, with perhaps one or two observers sitting at the back of the room. The premises must be dissociated from courts or police stations. Some hearings dispense with the table and sit quite informally.

PROCEDURE

Before the substantive consideration begins the child and his parents must accept the grounds for referral. If they do not, the hearing must either discharge the referral or have the case referred to the sheriff to establish the facts. This follows out the Kilbrandon concept that the hearing must concern itself only with the consideration of what action should be taken to help the child. The establishment of the facts is a matter for the sheriff (in civil procedure in chambers but with criminal standards of proof). If the facts are established, the case comes back to the hearing for consideration.

The hearing is then required to consider the grounds for referral, the report obtained from the social work department, and other relevant information that may be available. The hearing panel then considers on what course it should decide in the best *interests of the child.* This is the sole criterion to which the hearing is required to address itself. In the course of the proceedings, the hearing has to have as full a discussion as possible with the parents and the child. The aim is to be informal enough to enable a proper exchange of views to take place over a reasonable period. In practice, each hearing seems to average about 40 minutes. As will be seen, the procedure is very simple. There are a number of requirements, although to state them flatly does not reflect the full degree of discussion that usually takes place. The parents and the child must obviously have their say in the whole situation, including the discussion on disposal. The chairman must indicate the substance of the background report except where he considers it may be detrimental to the interests of the child. The chairman must subsequently record reasons for the disposal, and he can be asked to send these to the parents and the child (primarily for appeal purposes); and he must inform both parents and child of their rights of appeal.

More indicative of the flavor of a hearing is an account of the lines a hearing might often take. It would start off with introductions by the chairman, who would then proceed to establish beyond doubt, though not by formal plea, that the grounds for referral, namely the details of offenses or of a neglect situation are accepted. The parents and child will have had copies of these a week before. If they are accepted, there would be general discussion, usually commencing with the grounds but broadening out to the general situation. In due course this will come to a stage where possible disposals are canvassed, and then the chairman will indicate the hearing's decision—all within the open hearing.

DECISIONS

In form the hearing does not have a wide range of decisions available to it, though the powers can be flexibly used to insure that the treatment facilities available can be used to help the child.

1. It may decide that compulsory measures of care are not required and discharge the referral.
2. It may make a supervision requirement requiring a child to be supervised in the community. (Conditions may be included in the requirements; but the major use of this is to impose a condition about residence) (e.g., in a relative's home). Supervision might be defined as a statutory method of producing for a child a treatment program in the community.
3. It may make a supervision requirement requiring a child to reside in a "residential establishment." In effect, this means a local authority or voluntary establishment. Children's hearings in 1974 discharged over 6,000 (42%) and made over 7,000 (47%) (1.3 per 1,000 population) supervision requirements in the community and about 1,600 (11%) (0.3 per 1,000 population) involving residence away from home in a residential establishment.

In the crucial area of decision-making the hearing is required to have regard only to what is in the best interests of the child. It is not asked to concern itself with the possible "interests of the community," which could involve the removal of a child to a residential establishment for the community's protection or as a deterrent. There is good statistical and impressionistic evidence that reporters and hearings do consider the best interests of the child. Compulsory care is imposed in a minority of cases, and frequently there are distinctions in disposals made between children whose offenses are of a similar nature, which reflects the specific attention being paid to the individual. Just as, however, reporters refer children more readily for repeated offenses, even minor ones, so hearings in the case of continuing offenders may seem to operate a tariff system from discharge, to supervision in the community, to a residential disposal, to a secure place in a residential establishment. This may, of course, reflect not only a reluctant recognition of society's needs but also a considered attempt at an approach to treatment within the community before arriving at the ultimate residential-disposal approach, which tends to carry a gloomy prognosis for an effective return to the community.

The hearing is also inevitably concerned only with the individual child in what is a treatment situation. The diversion process cannot filter off all those whose problems are to a large extent the result of the multiple deprivation experienced by many in some of the large urban areas. But neither is the hearing likely to solve them by itself. It can, however, produce conditions for humane consideration and disposal of the cases with which it has to deal.

THE ROLE OF THE SHERIFF COURT

In addition to dealing directly with the special categories of cases mentioned earlier, the sheriff court is involved in establishing the facts of cases referred to it by the hearings, and in hearing appeals against decisions.

The sheriff court deals with the establishment of facts where grounds for referral are denied before the hearing and the hearing decides to ask the sheriff to establish the facts. This happens in only about 10 percent of the cases brought before the hearings.

The decisions made by a hearing may be appealed to the sheriff court and from there to the court of sessions on a point of law or irregularity. There are only a handful of appeals to the sheriff court, perhaps due to the ample provisions for review of the decision, an aspect discussed in Part III.

PART III

POST-HEARING

INTRODUCTION

If the children's hearings are essentially concerned with treatment, then treatment is what matters about the posttrial situation. This part of the chapter is initially concerned therefore with treatment resources both residential and nonresidential, although it also deals with the reviews which are such an integral part of the system.

It is plain that the slow development of resources is one of the major problems the new system faces (although it is not perhaps such a great danger to the system as the modern desire that every change should be an instant panacea). Arguably, this slow development is inevitable. Unless new development gains policy acceptance at national and local level, is enshrined in statute to achieve the necessary authority, takes its new place in the line for allocation of resources, and works its way through the long period required for the production of workers and of fabric, it has little chance of succeeding in its claims for resources or of ever getting off the ground at all. Legislation tends inevitably to be indicative legislation, and to be a beginning and not an end.

RESOURCES

At any rate, residential and nonresidential resources are in short supply. While authorities have been developing a range of children's homes and hearings have been sending children there and to foster homes, there has been a continuing shortage of suitable accommodation for maladjusted children. The result has been considerable additional pressure on the main residential resource, the schools formerly known as approved schools. These schools, of which there are twenty-six, are almost all run by voluntary managers and are financed jointly by the local authorities and the central government. Although they are known as schools, the main emphasis is not on education alone but on personal inner growth and social education; thus, they take their place in the range of facilities that local authorities have to provide to cover the needs of children. Since 1971 the schools have become more specifically individual in character; they have better staff-pupil ratios with more social workers and therapeutic input; and their regimes vary. But in practice they are still divided into age, sex, and religious groups in such a way as to make choice of placement limited, particularly in view of the waiting lists. The government has decided that the present system of financing the schools, whereby the cost is shared between the Exchequer and the local authorities, should cease; and a government decision is awaited on how the schools should be administered in the future, and whether schools of the present type are really required; it may be that a wider range of locally based establishments is what is required. The case is being pressed, however, for at least a small increase in the handful of secure places at present available for children for whom containment is necessary part of therapy. List D schools are not penal institutions; they are open establishments, and the children enjoy frequent home leave. There are, however, secure wings at two of the schools designed for the more difficult children for mplacement in the open school is not considered appropriate.

The main disposal alternative is supervision. At present the degree of supervision is for the local authority to decide, subject to any express conditions laid down by the children's hearing.

105

The possibility of stating in regulations what the supervision of a child should involve, in terms of minimum frequency of visits and other matters, is at present under consideration. In the context of the new expectations aroused by the Social Work (Scotland) Act, there is considerable pressure on social workers, and many children's panels feel a greater degree of supervision would be desirable than it is frequently possible to give in view of present staffing levels.

One development which has the merit both of helping to develop proper treatment programs for the children concerned and of enlisting extra resources is "intermediate treatment." This omnibus term is borrowed from England, but unlike the specific sentence there which underpins intermediate treatment, in Scotland it is simply a development of supervision, whereby structured educational, recreational, or therapeutic activities (e.g., involving group work) are made available.

The programs may involve weekend or very short residential elements. Nearly all regions have programs of this kind of a greater or lesser degree of sophistication, and there is increasing emphasis on the value of such enriched supervision in keeping children within the community, which is, of course, the broad aim of policy where feasible.

REVIEWS

An outstanding feature of the new system is the provision for reviews, which the greater input of resources into numbers of panel members and material for the hearings make possible. Unlike the previous court system where appeal was a matter for parent or child to pursue and was a formidable task, there is provision for a review after six months if requested by parents or child, or three months after a change of disposal. More important, there is a full review by a children's hearing each year which parents have the right to attend and which, except perhaps in long-term placements, the child would also attend. This hearing may discharge, continue, or vary the supervision requirement, and the latter is frequently done. While the Children Act of 1975 now makes a six-month case review by a local authority for children in the care of the local authority an essential part of the child-care process, the annual review by a children's hearing of cases of compulsory care is both a safeguard and an opportunity to try a new treatment program.

CONCLUSION

The children's hearing system has achieved the immediate aim of the Kilbrandon recommendations—that of diverting most cases involving children from the court and of relieving the court system of the necessity of the time-absorbing weight of legal consideration and argument. Instead, the children are considered by a lay panel which could claim to be more appropriate to the consideration of the essentially human and family welfare matters which are at the core of most issues coming before them. In its procedures at the hearing the system has won commendation for its humanity and respect for the dignity of the parents and the child. It is often able to effect true dialogue with parents and child that deals with the core issues instead of with the sometimes arbitrary example of social misbehavior which occasioned the appearance of the family and the child before the hearing. The reviews have allowed useful changes of direction in treatment to take place as they become indicated by developments in the child and his situation.

More broadly, the hearings themselves, since they are made up of groups of people from the local area, have come to realize that the majority of the children who appear before them come from personal situations and geographic locations known for the multiple deprivation experienced by many in some of the large urban areas. They come from poverty and often live in large housing schemes built with minimal amenities and isolated by poor transportation systems. The panel members' concern with this and with the general shortage of treatment resources has resulted in greater public knowledge and discussion of these issues than before, and there has thus been publicity for improvement. The irony is that some of the media have tended to link the shortage of resources with the system itself and to criticize the system, therefore blunting the impact of these new community insights. Hopefully, the panel's identification of the needs and the resultant publicity will help achieve an additional aim—that the public itself will become sufficiently concerned, to devote additional resources to the social and educational sector so that the children's needs will be more appropriately served.

For the future, better staffing and residential resources should lead to a system geared more to the individual child, and many of the children may be able to be dealt with by social work departments on referral from the reporter. As the social work departments themselves grow to their role, their normal routine coverage should reach some families or they would receive the cases on self-referral from the families or from the school. At the moment, the major source of referral to the reporter is from the police. This could be of help in the situation without the intervention of the hearing but additionally could refer cases to the social work department on a voluntary basis with increasing confidence. Similarly, the courts themselves may gain greater confidence in the ability of the hearings system to deal with the cases which might otherwise result in penal sentences. It is possible that in those cases where the court continues to sentence there may grow a pattern of combining the court hearing with ongoing supervision by the children's hearing. The current central influence on the panel system could decline as the system gains in ability and maturity and the system becomes even more obviously a local system, that is, a welfare board similar to the Scandinavian examples.

In the shorter term, however, while resources remain scarce

and the hearing's decision represents a narrow range of choice there will continue to be discussion about extra powers children's hearings might be given. For example, in some quarters, though not in others, there is suggestion that parents should find security for good behavior and that youths over sixteen still under supervision should be remitted to the sheriff for disposal. The extent to which this trend is likely to develop will be in inverse ratio to the rate at which the social work departments find themselves able to provide the treatment resources on which the ultimate success of the hearings depends.

There are two situations which the work of the panels cannot affect directly but which it is useful to bring into any discussion of the system. One affects the police responsibility, and the other the impact of the panel system on the local area culture and condition which may be the strongest influence affecting the appearance of the child and his family before the hearings. The Kilbrandon recommendations and similar advocates of "diversion" include, at least by implication, a belief that society need not be too concerned about "subserious" social misbehavior, particulry when, as in children, most of it is part of the growth process. But the change from court to hearing system as a method of juvenile justice does not involve any change in the responsibility of the police for law and order even though the police also have a "sifting" procedure for children. (Police community-involvement branch officers sift all police reports on children and make appropriate recommendation for warning by a superintendent. This formal warning may, with the consent of the parents, be followed by a short period of supervision by the officers.) However, in Scotland, as in other countries where there has been a move from a court system to a welfare-dominated system of juvenile justice, there has until recently been little recognition of the significance of the lack of coincidence between the basis of the system on which the police operate and the basis of the system on which the children's panel operates. The instructions through the children's panel are to be concerned only with those situations sufficiently serious to justify compulsory measures of care with all this means in diminution of free choice and liberty and sometimes actual removal from home. This responsibility need not coincide with the level of activity which the police, in pursuance of their law-and-order responsibility, might well find serious. A survey to see how this particular issue is resolved in the countries which followed this particular example of "diversion" in the juvenile justice field would be of interest. It would be particularly interesting to study the issue in metropolitan areas, which are traditionally associated with a higher incidence of juvenile misbehavior than more rural, less densely populated areas. If attention could be given to meeting this lack of coincidence of the roles of two public institutions—the police and the hearing—there will be more chance of the public being able to evaluate the wisdom of the current arrangements fairly. Police concern about law and order always makes good copy, and the publicity for the episodes with which the panels have no authority to deal is often inadequately handled and appears to be criticism of the panel system itself. This does less than justice to the desire of the police to handle questions of juvenile disorder sensibly or to the concern of the panel system for peaceful communities and the treatment of individual children.

7

Juvenile Justice in Yugoslavia

Alenka Šelih

BASIC CHARACTERISTICS OF THE JUVENILE JUSTICE SYSTEM IN YUGOSLAVIA

Before touching upon the central issue of how to deal with juvenile delinquency, I propose to deal briefly with the general features of the system qua system as well as with the ways and means used in that system. I shall, therefore, deal at first with the categories of juveniles, with different kinds of behavior that may bring a juvenile to the attention of the juvenile court or some other authority, with the agencies that deal with juvenile delinquents, and with their powers within this field. Finally, I shall try to give a brief survey of the extent of the juvenile delinquency.

JUVENILE AGE CATEGORIES

As far as the age categories of the juveniles are concerned, Yugoslavia has adopted a very restricted juvenile court jurisdiction. When adopted in 1960 it was certainly under the influence of the idea of humanization and treatment of offenders as promoted after World War II by the *defense sociale* movement. Accordingly, minors up to fourteen years of age (called *children*) do not fall within the scope of the juvenile court jurisdiction, and are not dealt with by any court. Minors over fourteen and under sixteen years of age at the time the offense has been committed are the first category which can be disposed of by the juvenile court and are designated *younger minors*. The second category to which special provisions regarding minors are applied are those who were over sixteen years of age at the time of the offense but who have not yet reached eighteen years of age and are designated *older minors*. The legal status of both categories differs to some extent. In the case of the younger minors, only educational measures and no penalties can be applied, whereas in the case of older minors, one special penalty, called *imprisonment for juveniles*, can also be imposed.

FORMS OF DELINQUENT BEHAVIOR

The intervention of the juvenile court has always been thought of as the last resort among different interventions on behalf of the juveniles. Therefore, only a relatively narrow scope of forms of behavior has been taken into account for judicial intervention: a minor can in fact be brought before the court only if he committed one of the offenses defined by the Criminal Code. But even so, one could argue that some of the offenses (e.g., petty theft, game poaching, fish poaching) need not necessarily be dealt with by juvenile courts if committed by minors.

The Criminal Code, however, does not include offenses such as petty traffic violations, disorderly conduct in public, and the like; in short, all that is called *petty offenses* and is dealt with by a special agency, the so-called *petty offense judge*. The Criminal Code does not include forms of misbehavior known in the Anglo-American law as juvenile status offenses.

The decision to limit the court's intervention is based on the assumption that agencies other than courts should deal with minors who have manifested their deviance, not by committing a criminal offense, but by other kinds of deviant behavior.

112

AGENCIES DEALING WITH MINORS

Actually, three agencies have to be taken into consideration as those which deal with problem children who are minors, according to the forms of their deviance.

Since the intervention of the juvenile court is reserved only for those between fourteen and eighteen years of age at the time they committed the offense, other agencies are supposed to act when younger age groups are concerned or forms of deviant behavior other than criminal offenses are in question.

SOCIAL-WELFARE AGENCIES

These agencies have been conceived as those which should have the first contact with children and minors showing troubles in their behavior or personality. Consequently, these agencies are responsible for dealing with every child under fourteen years of age who shows such difficulties as poor school performance, absconding from school, running away from home, or if the minor has done what would be a criminal offense if committed by an adult. These agencies, whose staff includes above all social workers and psychologists, have the right to apply any measure they deem necessary or appropriate for the child's education and benefit. They may work with the child in his normal environment (individual social work, casework, or group work), but they are also entitled to send the child to an appropriate institution if his further education requires it. The parents have, however, the right to appeal against such a decision if they do not agree with it.

In addition, these agencies deal with minors (from fourteen to eighteen years) who prove to have troubles not amounting to a criminal offense or petty offense. In that case they have the same rights as in regard of children. When they act on their own authority, in their daily performance, these agencies more often deal with those under fourteen years of age. However, they are also the agencies which implement certain educational measures ordered by the courts on behalf of juveniles.

PETTY OFFENSE JUDGES

The second type of agency dealing with minors is the so-called *petty offense judge*. Petty offenses are minor violations of public discipline, mainly traffic violations where not even a slight injury results, and certain forms of disorderly conduct. The procedure for dealing with petty offenses and the measures to be imposed on behalf of the minors in cases where they have committed a petty offense are in federal jurisdiction and therefore differ from one state to another. In Slovenia, the most northern of the Yugoslav republics, a petty offense judge can order either one of the educational measures (e.g., a kind of probation) or, for senior minors, a fine or short-term imprisonment (up to two months).

JUVENILE COURTS

There are no separate juvenile courts in Yugoslavia. There exist, however, special juvenile sections in the communal and district courts that hear the juvenile cases. The communal courts have jurisdiction over cases where the penalty is up to five years of strict imprisonment or milder, and the district courts have jurisdiction in all other cases—where a penalty heavier than five years of strict imprisonment is on the books for adults.

In the communal courts, the public prosecutor has, in the pretrial proceedings for juveniles, limited discretion to dismiss a case. There are two particular reasons for him to act like this: in cases where the penalty prescribed for adults is up to three years of imprisonment, he can dismiss the case if he reasonably believes that the criminal prosecution will be inexpedient in the light of the nature of the offense, the circumstances attending its commission, the minor's past conduct, and his personal attributes (art. 429, Code of Criminal Procedure); he also has the right to dismiss cases of minor importance which he deems of *insignificant social danger* (art. 4 sec. 2, Criminal Code). In the pretrial procedure, the judge for juveniles also has the right to dismiss a case. He can act so if the public prosecutor, during the preparatory proceedings, submits to discontinue them and if it appears to the judge that there are in fact no grounds for continuing them. Here again, reasons such as inexpediency, negligible social danger of the offense and of the offender are taken into account.

While handling the juvenile cases, the public prosecutor, as well as the judge, often makes use of these special provisions, so that a large portion of juveniles is dealt with in other ways without an educational measure being imposed by the court.

THE EXTENT OF THE JUVENILE DELINQUENCY[1]

It follows from what had been said that the notion of juvenile delinquency in Yugoslavia is a vary narrow one and that the system adopted in the early 1960s was one in which the intervention of the juvenile court was limited to the narrow field of jurisdiction that had been traditional in the country before this system came into being. So, without even knowing about *diversion* and its techniques and possibilities, there has been a trend to keep children and juveniles out of the criminal justice system, in the belief that this could be a stigmatizing as well as traumatizing experience.

To give an idea of the extent of what is officially labeled juvenile delinquency, we refer to the data in Table 1.

---

1. All statistical data were extracted from *Statistical Yearbook of Yugoslavia,* 1971, 1972, 1973, 1974, 1975, Beograd, Savezni zavod za statistiku.

TABLE 1

JUVENILES TOWARD WHOM EDUCATIONAL MEASURES WERE
USED BECAUSE OF PERPETRATED OFFENSES
(YUGOSLAVIA, 1971-75)*

	YEAR					%
Kind of Uses	1971	1972	1973	1974	1975	1971–75
against life and limb (violence)	573	615	552	602	498	7.2
against property	6488	7324	5910	6559	6132	85.0
other	502	626	613	698	556	7.8
total	7563	8586	7075	7859	7196	100.0

The figures represented in the table refer to the last five years
for which data were available. The ratios of the perpetrated offenses do not seem to vary greatly during this time period.

Compared to many other countries, these figures certainly are
low and the number of delinquent juveniles per 100,000 population between fourteen and eighteen is 490. However, they
show—in spite of the decreases in 1973 and 1975—a tendency
toward an increase and this tendency can be noted even more if a
longer time span is taken into consideration.[2] It is this tendency

---

2. Cf. Katja Vodopivec, "Criminological Diagnosis in
Yugoslavia," Institute of Criminology at the Faculty of
Law, University of Ljubljana, Ljubljana 1973, pp. 44-45
(mimeographed).
Tihomir Vasiljevic, *The Causes of Failure to prevent
Juvenile Delinquency in Yugoslavia,* Zbornik radova,
Pravni fakultet u Novom Sadu, 1971, pp. 130 ff.

as well as its dynamic nature that causes much of the concern about juvenile delinquency.

A better insight in the problem can be gained if it is taken into consideration that pursuant to the data gathered: in 1975, 14,233 criminal offenses committed by juveniles were reported either to the police or to the public prosecutor. In 9,823 cases the public prosecutor motioned the juvenile court to apply one of the educational measures; the courts applied such a measure in cases of 7,196 juveniles. The offenses most frequently committed by

TABLE 2

THE KINDS OF EDUCATIONAL MEASURES APPLIED
ON BEHALF OF JUVENILES (YUGOSLAVIA, 1975)*

Educational Measures	1975	%	
reprimand	1993	27.6	
disciplinary center	258	3.7	Non-institutional
strict supervision by parents or foster family	1515	21.0	6141 or 85%
strict supervision by the social welfare agency	2375	33.0	
educational institution	315	4.4	
educational-reformatory institution	556	7.8	
			Institutional
juvenile imprisonment	169	2.3 .	1055 or 15%
other	15	0.2	
total	7196	100.0	

*All data in this and in following tables have been taken from the publication *STATISTICKI GODISNJAK JUGOSLAVIJE* (statistical yearbook of Yugoslavia) which appears yearly and contains data for the year preceding the year of publication.)

juveniles are offenses against property (85%), among which theft, burglary, and joyriding are the most frequent, while offenses associated with violence are much lower (about 7.8%). Another feature that can be of interest are the measures applied on behalf of juveniles.

The data in this table show that noninstitutional measures, that is, those during the implementation of which the juvenile stays at home in his normal environment, are the most frequently applied. Among the noninstitutional measures, the strict supervision of social welfare agencies is the most frequent.[3] This measure—in spite of all the deficiencies associated with its implementation—is the one which offers opportunities for treatment in the family setting.

We could conclude that, in spite of the fact that juvenile delinquency does not represent an immediate social danger, it should be considered a serious problem of increasing complexity. Although relatively small in number (in the light of court data), juvenile delinquency seems to be a complex problem, if those children and juveniles who have shown deviant behavior but have not been dealt with by judicial authorities are taken into account.

FORMS OF DIVERSION

In using the word "diversion," I do not refer to any particular new trend that might have been noticed recently. And I certainly do not use it because it has recently become fashionable.

It will be noticed from what has already been said that the system described tries to restrict the juvenile court intervention for cases which are the most serious as far as the form of the deviant behavior involved is concerned.

Thus, none of those under fourteen years of age ever enters the juvenile justice system. The same is true of the so-called

---

3. This measure is very close to probation.

juvenile status offenses, which are never—regardless of the age of the perpetrator—dealt with by the court.

Finally, juveniles (from fourteen to eighteen years of age) that have committed petty offenses are also dealt with outside the juvenile court system.

In all these cases, agencies other than juvenile courts take care of children and juveniles. But one cannot accept this solution without questioning it. Such children and juveniles do not enter the judicial system, but on the other hand, they do enter some other system (social welfare agencies, petty offense judges), and it is open to see what kind of stigma is attached to those who have been dealt with by those other agencies and what kind of treatment they receive.

Within the scope of diversion techniques, the two forms of dismissing a juvenile have already been mentioned and have also to be taken into consideration. These are the discretionary powers accorded to the public prosecutor and to the judge for the juveniles to dismiss a case before adjudication within the limits of the special prerogatives given to both of these offices (insignificant social danger of the offense and of the offender, the so-called *principe d'opportunite*).

PRE-TRIAL AND TRIAL PROCEEDINGS

In presenting a survey of these proceedings, I shall mainly refer to the juvenile court proceedings, leaving aside the peculiarities of the proceedings before the petty offense judge or before the social welfare agencies.

THE PRE-TRIAL PROCEEDINGS

The public prosecutor is the only one who can initiate such proceedings. Before proposing the initiation, he has the right to dismiss the case as described above. It is the judge for juveniles who conducts the pretrial proceedings. Great emphasis is laid upon collecting data on the juvenile's personality, his family background and school performance, his earlier development, and so on. The offense is considered—theoretically at least—only as a symptom of his personal or environmental difficulties. While gathering the data about the offense, the judge is also supposed to secure a detailed analysis of the juvenile's personality and his environment. Social inquiry is usually carried out by the social welfare agencies (usually by a social worker), or, when they are available, by social workers attached to the court.

During these proceedings, the judge is entitled to send the juvenile to an observation center; he may place the youth under the supervision of the social welfare agency; or he may send him to an educational institution to secure him shelter, care, and protection. Usually, however, the juvenile is released to the custody of his parents. According to the law, the judge may exceptionally hold the juvenile in preventive detention. The courts, however, seem to use preventive detention so often that one could hardly say it is used "exceptionally" only. According to recent research, the juvenile courts in Slovenia used it in dealing with 20 percent of all juveniles.[4]

The main feature which differs the juvenile pretrial proceedings from those against adults is the cooperation in them of the social welfare agency. This agency, through its social worker, prepares what is called a *social report* on the juvenile. It contains data on his family and school environment, on his response to these environments, on his deficiencies, on his

---

4. Cf. Katja Vodopivec et al., "The Role of the Public Prosecutor and the Counsel for Defence in the Criminal Proceedings on behalf of Juveniles" (mimeographed), Institute for Criminology at the Faculty of Law, University of Ljubljana, 1974, p. 65 and app. 15.
   Cf. Danica Marinkovic-Pejovic, *Application of Measures to Secure the Presence of the Juvenile in the Criminal Proceedings and the Efficacy of Criminal Proceedings,* Jugoslovenska revija za kriminologiju i krivicno pravo, Beogard 1969, pp. 451 ff.

potential special interests, and on his peer groups and his attitudes toward them. Such a report sometimes also contains a proposal to the court concerning the kind of measure which should be applied on behalf of the juvenile. These reports are supposed to be of great value to the judge and to the juvenile panel for their decision.

Since the *parens patriae* philosophy has never been accepted in the proceedings on behalf of juveniles in Yugoslavia, the same safeguards are applied to minors as to the adults in respect to the right to be represented by a fully qualified and practicing attorney from the first hearing on. He has to be represented by an attorney if the charge is heavier, so that the case is to be handled not by communal, but by district court. Before being interrogated, he must be informed of this right, and a note on the point must be made in the minutes. The courts, however, seem to be inclined toward appointing defense counsels *ex officio* at the time of fixing the main trial.[5]

THE COURT TRIAL

After the pretrial proceedings have been completed, the file is returned to the public prosecutor, who may either propose to discontinue the proceedings or set forth the *reasoned motion* which is a kind of charge. After receiving it, the judge for juveniles starts with the preparations for the main trial or for the session of the juvenile panel.

The panel which is to make the decision consists of the judge for juveniles (who is a law graduate and the chairman of the panel) and of two assessors[6] who have experience in work with youth. The juvenile panel can take the decision on behalf of the juvenile either at its session or at the main trial. At the session of the juvenile panel, only noninstitutional measures can be ap-

---

5. Cf. K. Vodopivec et al., op. cit., 1974, app. 13.
6. For more serious offenses the panel consists of 2 judges and lawyers and 3 assessors.

plied. Those taking part in it: the members of the panel, the public prosecutor, the defense counsel, and the representative of the social welfare agency. The juvenile himself is absent and is called in afterward by the judge who explains to him the measure ordered on his behalf.

The courts differ considerably as far as the use of such a session is concerned. The study cited above shows that in Slovenia some district courts dealt with as many as 56% of juvenile cases through the Sessions, while some did not use it at all. The frequent use of such sessions raises the question of how the courts protect the principle that the juvenile is to be present when adjudicated.[7]

Usually, however, the cases are decided following the main trial. The public is excluded from the trial. The pretrial proceedings as well as the main trial are, in juvenile cases, handled by the same judge. This practice is supposed to provide for the judge's better understanding of the whole situation and should give him a full insight into the needs of the juvenile in order that the decision to be arrived at would achieve, at the best, both goals—the juvenile's rehabilitation and the society's need for protection.

The main trial serves two purposes. Firstly, it must be proven that it was the "accused juvenile" who perpetrated the offense; and secondly, the juvenile's personality, and his environment's potential deficiencies have to be established, and the needs for his future reeducation and rehabilitation stated. To this end, special information will have been gathered during the preparatory proceedings (social inquiry, other expert opinions). In addition, the juvenile's parents, who are free not to testify as far as the offense is concerned, are bound to testify about the juvenile's previous life and his development, behavior, interests, and so on.

----

7. Cf. K. Vodopivec et al., op. cit., 1974, app. 17.

THE IMPLEMENTATION OF
EDUCATIONAL MEASURES

There are special measures for juveniles in the Criminal Code. Except for one penalty—juvenile imprisonment—the rest of them are educational measures. But even juvenile imprisonment is close to educational measures, since it is similar to them in many respects. It will, therefore, be described along with them.

Noninstitutional Measures. The Code provides for two so-called *disciplinary measures* which are to be applied to a minor who needs not be submitted to an extended educational or reformatory measure, and particularly to one who has committed a criminal offense out of thoughtlessness or frivolity (art. 70, Criminal Code). *Reprimand* is rather frequently delivered, although it seems to have no special effect whatsoever. It is, however, the first measure to be applied. It is probably used in too many cases.[8]

The second disciplinary measure is *commitment to a disciplinary center for minors* which could be applied in three different forms: (1) for several hours per day during a one-month period; (2) for a specified number of hours on holiday, on not more than four consecutive holidays; or (3) for a continuous stay over a specified number of days, totaling no more than twenty days (art. 72, Criminal Code). This measure, introduced by the Code in 1960, has never been fully accepted by the courts, and only a small number of juveniles are sent to a disciplinary center. Among different forms in which this measure can be implemented only the first one is in fact applied. In spite of the fact that data were collected on the ways this

---

8. Cf. Desanka Lazarevic, *The Role of Legal Institutions in the Prevention of Juvenile Delinquency,* Zbornik Instituta za kriminoloska i socioloska istrazivanja, Beograd 1972, I. no. 1, p. 196.

measure is carried out and on the possibilities it offers, the courts don't seem to have accepted it.[9]

The second group of the noninstitutional measures is the *strict supervision*, which, too, can be applied in different forms—as *strict supervision either by parents, by a foster family, or by social welfare agencies*. The judge will order these measures if it appears necessary to submit the minor to extended measures of education or reformation when there is no need to tear him out of his environment (art. 70, Criminal Code). The last of these three forms of strict supervision is the most frequently used by the courts. It is generally admitted that it probably offers the best possibilities for treatment of a juvenile in a noninstitutional setting, but it has also been established that it is applied in cases in which the deficiencies of the juvenile would require a more severe reeducational setting. Therefore, the probability of a failure is much greater in such cases.[10]

The *strict supervision by parents* ought to be applied in cases in which the parents prove to be capable of providing a stricter supervision of the juvenile than they did before. However, the court may order the social welfare agency to control or supervise the implementation of the supervision as carried out by the parents. The problem which had been noticed in this connection in the everyday work of these agencies has been the delimitation between this kind of supervision and the supervision carried out by social welfare agencies themselves. It occurs sometimes that the control in the strict supervision by parents takes nearly the same forms as the supervision by the social welfare agencies themselves.

---

9. Cf. Ante Caric: *Committal to the Disciplinary Center for Juveniles,* Kriminalisticko-kriminoloski institut "Ivan Vucetic" pri pravnom fakultetu u Splitu, Split 192, 99 pp.
10. Cf. Bronislav Skaberne et al., *An Evaluation of Probation in the Republic of Slovenia,* Institut za kriminologijo pri pravni fakulteti v Ljubljana, Ljubljana, 1969, pp. 52-57.

Among the different kinds of strict supervision measures, the *strict supervision by a foster family* is applied very seldom. Although there is a tradition of having children in foster families, it is hard to find a family that would be ready to accept a delinquent minor who may require more help and understanding than a nondelinquent child and may, in spite of all this, show no improvement.

The duration of the educational measure of strict supervision is prescribed by the Code and may not be shorter than one year nor longer than three years. In a particular case, the length is not determined by the court at the time when it is imposed. It is determined during its implementation according to the results, but it can in no case take longer than three years.

The Institutional Measures. The Criminal Code provides for three kinds of institutional measure: (1) *the commitment to an educational institution*; (2) *commitment to an educational reformatory home*; and (3) *commitment to an institution for defective minors*. Besides these three measures, the *juvenile imprisonment*, that is, a penalty, can be imposed.

The educational institutions are actually of two types. There are those that house neglected chidren and children in need of care under the age of fourteen, and there are those that house minors older than fourteen years. In the latter case, minors could either be delinquent and hence sent to the institution by the juvenile court, or nondelinquent and hence sent to it by the social welfare agencies because of being in need of care, being incorrigible, and so on. This of course, means that an educational institution for minors from fourteen to eighteen can house a mixed population of delinquent as well as nondelinquent youths. However, since the criminal offense is supposed to be only a symptom of the minor's personality or his behavior troubles, this should not influence their treatment. The Criminal Code provides for the minimum duration of this measure at six months and the maximum at three years, and the court determines it during the implementation according to the results yielded.

The educational reformatory institutions are intended for delinquent minors only. In selecting this measure, the court considers particularly the gravity and the nature of the offense and whether the juvenile has already been subjected to educational measures and/or to punishments. This actually is the only educational measure for the application of which the Code sets forth the criterion referring to the gravity of the offense and to the minor's previous court history. According to these criteria, the educational reformatory institutions accept minors with a longer previous delinquent record, presumably showing more deficiencies in behavior and personality than minors in educational institutions. However, a study has recently shown that several personality traits in youths in an educational reformatory institution in one of the Yugoslav republics (Slovenia) were very close to the youths in three other educational institutions in the same republic.[11] The length of the sentence to an educational reformatory institution is not less than one year and not more than five years.

Committal to an institution for defective minors was introduced into the Criminal Code in 1960 as the result of these measures. It was supposed to be used on behalf of those minors who are handicapped (deaf, blind, etc.), mentally ill, or psychically underdeveloped. This measure is ordered in lieu of committal to another institution and should provide for custody and care of such minors. However, it is very rarely used by courts, not because there is no need for committals, but because of the lack of suitable facilities. Besides, the main category of minors who are in need of such a special treatment are those who show serious personality disorders and are therefore not capable

----

11. Cf. Vinko Skalar, *Social Climate in the Experimental and Control Institutions,* in Katja Vodopivec (ed.); *Maladjusted Youth,* Saxon House/Lexington Books, Westmead, England, 1974, pp. 217-226.

of being dealt with in other institutions for minors. Unfortunately, the possiblities of dealing with them are scarce.

The last sanction provided for minors is the *penalty of juvenile imprisonment.* Although a penalty, juvenile imprisonment is, as far as the underlying philosophy is concerned, very close to educational measures, since the court is bound to take into consideration the minor's needs for education, reformation, and vocational training. The limits within which the court may inflict juvenile imprisonment are rather narrow and refer to the following conditions:

1. Only a senior minor (16 to 18 years of age) can be sentenced to this penalty.
2. The minor has to be found guilty.
3. The juvenile had committed an offense that had a penalty of more than five years' strict imprisonment if committed by an adult.
4. The educational measures would—because of the gravity of the offense and the high degree of criminal responsibility—not be warranted (art. 79c- 79f, Criminal Code).

The juvenile imprisonment is carried out in special institutions only for juveniles. Although most of these institutions are rather closed, emphasis is placed upon the reeducation of minors and upon their vocational training. The minimum length of the imprisonment is one year, and its maximum length is ten years.

Problems of Implementation. The system of educational measures for minors as described above was enacted by the Criminal Code in 1960. Since then it has shown probably both its strength as well as its weaknesses. We have already mentioned that since 1960 juvenile delinquency has been increasing, and this has been one of the main reasons for criticism of the system as a whole. However, it is open to question whether such criticisms are founded, since it could not have been proven that the increase could be attributed exclusively to the system introduced.

It is also interesting to see what changes have been brought about during this time span concerning the forms of educational measures which have been applied by the courts. For the sake of comparison, we have chosen a lapse of 10 years, 1965-75, to present the structure of measures the courts imposed. In 1965 the system which came into operation in 1960 had already settled down. On the other hand, 1975 was the last year for which data had been published at the time of the preparation of this report.

TABLE 3

THE KINDS OF EDUCATIONAL MEASURES APPLIED
ON BEHALF OF JUVENILES
(Yugoslavia, 1965 and 1975)

	YEAR		%	
Kind of Measure	1965	1975	1965	1975
reprimand	1010	1993	21.6	27.6
disciplinary center	222	258	4.7	3.7
strict supervision by parents or foster family	969	1515	20.9	21.0
strict supervision by social welfare agency	1457	2375	31.2	33.0
educational institution	243	315	5.2	4.4
educational-reformatory institution	673	556	14.2	7.8
juvenile imprisonment	90	169	1.9	2.3
other	18	15	0.3	0.2
total	4682	7196	100.0	100.0

The data indicate that a shift occurred from such sanctions which are rather repressive, or offer no or only few reeducational possibilities toward those which yield some reeducational or treatment chances. The ratio of institutional measures has become smaller, which means that on the one hand, services dealing with juveniles in noninstitutional settings have expanded and become able to deal with a greater number of such juveniles

128

who might have earlier been dealt with in institutional settings, while, on the other hand, the population of minors sent to institutions has grown more difficult and selected.

One of the important changes after the introduction of the new system is probably the one in methods applied with the reeducational work with minors. Social workers whose work expanded in general in the 1960s introduced their methods of work while working with minors. During the last decade, social work methods in dealing especially with minors under strict supervision have improved. The first trend was probably toward the casework methods, but within the last few years efforts have been made, at least in some of the republics, to make use of social group work as well.

It should be noticed, however, that the social welfare services have not succeeded in developing new or in expanding existing possibilities of reeducational work within the community settings. These settings offer, sometimes at least, such forms of work in which minors could be included along with the nondelinquent youth. There exist quite a number of different youth organizations which specialize in a particular field (sports associations, scouts, science for youth, mountain climbing, etc.) and would probably be both capable and willing to accept minors with personality or behavior difficulties—provided that special care, guidance, and the like, have been secured.

As for the institutional measures, a shift could be noticed, in some institutions at least, toward using permissive methods in dealing with juveniles. This especially holds true for educational institutions, and particularly in the republic of Slovenia. This shift followed an experiment carried out by the Institute of Criminology at the School of Law, University of Ljubljana, in one of the educational institutions in Slovenia.[12] In spite of

---

12. K. Vodopivec (ed.), *Malajusted Youth,* Saxon House/Lexington Books, Westmead, England, 1974, XII 275 pp.

many doubts, the experiment and the methods employed have been widely recognized.

IV. PROBLEMS AND PERSPECTIVES

In presenting the problems which arise from the situation as has been described, one is bound to make a personal choice and appraisal.

Whatever critical standpoints have been heard within the last few years in connection with the problem of juvenile delinquency, it must be stressed that there were no voices as to changing the bases of the system in any other, perhaps more repressive way.[13] It has been generally acknowledged that in spite of all of its deficiencies and shortages, the conception underlying the system as a whole is a sound and even a promising one. Its deficiencies have been found in different areas, and remedies for them have been sought for in equally different fields. We could perhaps select some of the problems

The first question which imposes itself refers to the time of intervention. The system which has been adopted presupposes that social welfare agencies would intervene with children under 14 years of age when they showed difficulties in behavior. An early intervention should facilitate the reeducation of the child, since presumably his troubles at this stage are smaller than after they have accumulated for several years. However, the social welfare agencies often delay the intervention until the child is 14 and the juvenile court has imposed a measure on his behalf.

A recent study in the Republic of Croatia has established that a great majority of children under 14 years of age who had committed a criminal offense had not come to the attention of the social welfare agencies; or if they did, the agencies did not act. It seems that these agencies have been given too many obligations and responsibilities without having, at the same time, enough

---

13. T. Vasiljevic, op. cit., pp. 143.

personnel and financial resources to carry them out. It is questionable, of course, whether an early intervention is always a proper solution, since in many cases the difficulty may pass over with time without any intervention at all. However, the ideology of nonintervention is not at the basis of the noninterventions of the social welfare agencies on behalf of children under 14 years of age.[14]

A similar problem is connected with the dismissed cases (dismissed either by the public prosecutor or by the juvenile court). These cases, too, are based on the presumption that the social welfare agencies would take care of the juvenile in question. The activity of these agencies here is very limited too. A study carried out on that point proved that the agencies did not act, in spite of having been informed about the dismissals, and in spite of the fact that the study showed a great number of personality or family problems. The social welfare service in general is of the opinion that in such cases the court has imposed a measure, and the agencies' intervention is based on the court authority.[15]

In the social welfare agencies, the proceedings which follow the Administrative Procedure Act are in some respects simpler

---

14. Cf. Magda Bayer et al., *Children under 14 years of Age—Perpetrators of Criminal Offences,* Pravni fakultet Sveucilista u Zagrebu, Zagreb, 1975, pp. 98-99; T. Vasiljevic, op. cit., pp. 113; Olga Matic, *"The Role of Social-Welfare Agencies in the Criminal Proceedings and in the process of Implementation of Measures Imposed upon Juvenile Delinquents,"* Jugoslovenska revija za krivicno pravo i kriminologiju, Beograd 9/1971, No. 1, pp. 43-49.
15. Cf. Joze Friedl et al., *"The Work of Social-Welfare Agencies with Juveniles after the Dismissal of Criminal Proceedings,"* Socijalna politika, Beograd 28/1973, No. 3, pp. 19-29.

than the proceedings in the juvenile court, since they do not include the same safeguards. Therefore, the possibility cannot be completely excluded that in these proceedings the situation of a minor or child is disadvantageous when compared with his situation in the court proceedings.

Still along with the line of the work of the social welfare agencies, it should be noted that social work has only a short professional tradition. Therefore, the problems related to the professional ethics of social workers have not been discussed so far, and little attention has been given to them. One of the recent studies shows, however, that this service pays too little attention to a possible stigmatization, not so much of the client himself, but of the persons who are not directly involved (e.g., parents, described as alcoholics in the criminal proceedings on behalf of their child).[16]

Another problem which should be mentioned is that of dealing with petty offenses committed by minors. As far as the proceedings are concerned, the same applies to them as to the proceedings with the social welfare agencies. They are prescribed by a special Law on Petty Offenses (separate for each republic). Although the proceedings are governed by the same principle as the criminal court proceedings, they are, to some degree, simplified in order to be more expedient. This may produce some drawbacks as far as the minor's safeguards are concerned. However, the main criticism[17] in this area has been directed toward the fact that minors dealt with by these agencies are treated much more repressively than they would be in the court for juveniles. Only some of the republics provide for the same (or nearly the same) educational measures for minors if they have committed a petty offense as if they have perpetrated a

---

16. Cf. K. Vodopivec et al., op. cit. 1973, pp. 89.
17. Cf. D. Lazarevic, op. cit., pp. 203-205; Alenka Selih, "Petty Offences Committed by Juveniles and the Ways of Dealing with Them," Revija za kriminalistiko in kriminologijo, 24/1973, No. 3, pp. 225.

criminal offense. Contrary to the tendencies of the Criminal Code, the petty offenses acts still prescribe fines and short-term imprisonment for minors. Therefore, the ways of dealing with minors who have committed a petty offense (which is a less serious violation than a criminal offense) seem to be inconsistent with the system dealing with juvenile delinquency in general. It is expected, however, that soon all the republics will legalize the possibility of also applying educational measures in these cases.

The next area of interest is the functioning of the system of educational measures for juveniles and the roles of the juvenile courts within it. One of the main criticisms here is directed at the fact that some of the educational measures, as set forth by the Criminal Code in 1960, can not even today be implemented properly, if at all. That holds true for the *commitment to the institution for defective youth* where claims are frequently made that an institution for a psychically disturbed delinquent youth would be urgently needed. However, while on the one hand the system of measures provided for by the law is fully accepted and raises fewer doubts or objections, on the other hand, it has been noted that the proceedings adopted on behalf of juveniles may prove to be more questionable.

These proceedings were adopted in the 1960's (as was the rest of the system) and were influenced by the ideas of treatment of juveniles and their reeducation. Following this perspective, the legislator also introduced certain solutions which may seem disadvantageous for the minor if compared to an adult. This, for example, is true when the juvenile panel is allowed legally to order a noninstitutional educational measure for the juvenile *in absentia*. Also, data about the juvenile's personality are being gathered in the pretrial proceedings, although the case may later be dismissed.[18]

18.Cf. Ante Caric, "New Tendencies in the Development of the Yugoslav Juvenile Justice System," Zbornik radova pravnog fakulteta u Splitu, Splint 11/1974, p. 44.

Let me finally turn to the implementation of educational measures; it has been a major target of critics in assessing the problems of juvenile delinquency in general.

It has frequently been emphasized that the deficiencies in the implementation of educational measures often compromise the juvenile justice system as a whole. The main objections were raised in the following directions: the social welfare agencies do not pay sufficient attention to the children under 14; that is, during the age when the child might be more responsive to reeducational efforts. Besides, these agencies are overloaded with different (and sometimes not clearly defined) tasks, which they are not altogether capable of carrying out, either because of the lack of personnel or of funds or because of not being experienced enough in the special field. Rather similar criticisms were raised on behalf of reeducation in institutions. It has also been pointed out that the system as a whole is badly coordinated and that the services of different agencies may sometimes overlap.[19]

19. Cf. T. Vasiljovic, op. cit., pp. 131.

8

The Swedish Approach to Juvenile Corrections

Ola Nyquist

In the handling of young offenders Sweden distinguishes between the following age groups: under fifteen; between fifteen
and eighteen; and over eighteen.

THE OFFENDER UNDER FIFTEEN

In Sweden the age of *criminal responsibility* is fifteen. This is
accordingly the age limit under which a young person cannot be
punished. He can be brought before a court having jurisdiction
in criminal matters[1] though, in the very rare case of securing and
considering matters of evidence. Young offenders under fifteen,
are, with this exception, exclusively dealt with by locally
established *social welfare boards*.

Up to 1970 there were in Sweden separate child welfare
boards, separate temperance boards, and separate social welfare
boards for, among other things, public assistance and the care of
old people. Since the middle of 1970 Sweden has integrated all
those boards into a central social welfare board system. In each

---

1. There are no special criminal and civil courts in Sweden, nor
   any special family or juvenile/youth courts.

135

local community (about 270 in all), there is a social welfare board working on the basis of *the family approach,* according to the principle of entirety. The boards, having a staff of professional social workers, are composed of at least nine laymen elected by the local government for a three-year period, working whenever feasible in a decentralized manner through fully staffed *district boards*. Also the district boards members—there should be at least five—are elected by the local government. At least one of the members of the district board must also be a member of the central board. In the city of Uppsala with about 150,000 inhabitants, as an example, there are four district boards each with its own personnel. Expert legal and medical knowledge should be represented on the boards whenever practicable. In the larger municipalities lawyers are appointed as secretaries on the boards.

THE OFFENDER BETWEEN FIFTEEN AND EIGHTEEN

For a number of reasons it is certainly justified to distinguish the age group fifteen to eighteen from other age groups. Besides the fact that the age of *civil majority* in Sweden is eighteen, the fifteen to eighteen year old age group and especially the fifteen-year-old ones, who have just left or are about to leave, the compulsory school system, shows a very high proportion of crime compared with other age groups. With regard to these offenders there is an overlapping jurisdiction for the social welfare system and the system of criminal justice. After hearing the social welfare board, it is in the discretion of the *chief public prosecutor* in each county (24 in all) to decide where the offender should be dealt with. The overwhelming number of cases are surrendered to the social welfare boards by way of dropping prosecution. If the prosecutor considers—because of public points of view—that he cannot waive prosecution, the case is brought before a court having jurisdiction in criminal matters.[2] This does not necessarily mean, however, that the offender is cut off from social welfare board measures. The court may—after having taken an affirmative stand in the adjudication matter—dispose of the case by referring it to the local social welfare board for *public care*.[3] As a matter of fact, this is very often done. Statistics show that the public prosecutors increasingly waive prosecution. In 1956 they dealt with about 4,000 young offenders aged fifteen to eighteen. Prosecution was dropped in about 80 percent of these cases. The rest were prosecuted and disposed of by the courts. In 1973 the total number of cases dealt with was about 9,000; about 90 percent were waived; about 10 percent were disposed of by the courts.

Of the 883 court cases in 1973, fourteen were sentenced to ordinary imprisonment; 18 were sentenced to youth prison; 116 were placed on probation; 101 were given a conditional sentence; and 634 (or 72%) were surrendered to the social welfare boards for requisite care. In many of these 634 cases, the courts, in addition to the surrender for public care, *imposed a fine* in accordance to the statutory rule empowering them to do so if deemed necessary for the correction of the offender or out of consideration for public law obedience.

THE OFFENDER OVER EIGHTEEN

As a general rule the *young adult offender* should be dealt with by the court. But also in these cases, if the offender is under twenty years of age the social welfare board has the competence to deal with the case. If so, this is done, not by means of a

---

2. In some of the larger cities, the courts have special juvenile sections.
3. On the various forms of public care.

137

waiver, but through prosecution and a court disposition. The young adult offender will be brought before the court and, after adjudication, surrendered to the social welfare board for public care. This is done, however, in comparatively few cases. Thus is 1973 the courts disposed of 3,286 cases of eighteen-to-twenty-year-old offenders in the following way: 889 were sentenced to ordinary imprisonment; 175 were sentenced to youth prison; 1,829 were placed on probation; 1,114 were given a conditional sentence; and 279 (or 8.5%) were surrendered to the social welfare boards for public care. Separately, 5,804 young adults were fined. The corresponding figure for the fifteen-to-eighteen-year-olds was 2,486.

JURISDICTION SUMMARIZED

Offenders under fifteen are dealt with exclusively by the social welfare boards.[4] So are, for the most part, those between fifteen and eighteen years of age, except for the trivial cases and some very serious cases. Very few juveniles are kept in prison. After the age of eighteen the young offenders are dealt with in much the same way as are the adults.

The jurisdiction of the social welfare boards is defined in section 25 of the Child Welfare Act of 1960. This section provides that the social welfare boards shall take action in the following circumstances:

---

4. As indicated above, the courts may look into the matter of evidence. Under section 13 of the Special Rules for Young Offenders (1964) the social welfare board may request a trial and a finding as to the question if the young person under fifteen in fact did commit the alleged offense. This is very seldom done.

(b) if a person, not yet eighteen years of age, needs special corrective measures by the community because of his criminal act, immoral manner of life, failure to support himself honestly according to his ability, misuse of intoxicating beverages or narcotics or for some other comparable reason

If a person referred to in (b) is guilty of a criminal act, no intervention in accord with this Act may be made, however, after he has reached eighteen years of age, unless his mode of life in other respects provides an adequate cause or such intervention must be considered most appropriate for his correction, in view of ongoing treatment under the present Act or some other special reason.

The commission of a criminal act alone is evidently not a sufficient requisite for action to be taken by the board. There must in addition be a need for special corrective measures. This fact is given special consideration when it comes to an intervention in the case of a young offender over eighteen years of age.

BOARD MEASURES

If circumstances referred to in section 25 of the Child Welfare Act are present, the social welfare board shall attempt, insofar as possible, to produce a remedy by one or more *preventive measures,* namely:

1. Aid, including advice and support (financial support, job or training arrangements, medical care and so forth).
2. Admonition and warning.
3. Directives concerning the young person's living conditions.
4. Supervision (probation).

If preventive measures are judged profitless or if such measures have been taken without resulting in correction, the young offender shall be taken in charge for *public care,* which means, generally speaking, that he shall be assigned to a private home (foster home) or be placed in a suitable institution. Institutional care for the most part means a placement in an approved school or a vocational school (= juvenile welfare schools). It does also imply a probational period outside the schools. Statistics show that the number of preventive measures has been cut down radically during the last years. In 1965 about 20,000 such measures were taken by the boards. The corresponding figure in 1973 was less than 13,000! Only from 1972 to 1973 did the number of admonitions and warnings drop from 818 to 542. The picture does not reflect a decline in juvenile crime. It rather shows that the preventive measures have not been found to be effective. The social welfare boards tend more and more to take no definite action at all. In about 20 percent of all cases the case is closed with reference to the fact that the investigation made is considered to be action enough. Less than 10 percent of the total number of cases were surrendered to public care.

The use of institutional care shows a parallel trend. The number of juvenile welfare schools is quite heavily reduced. And only from 1971 to 1973 did the intake decline about 35 percent, from 600 to 385 committed young persons. The situation also reflects a general disbelief also in current institutional measures. The high rate of recidivism, about 70 to 80 percent in the institutional cases, of course has contributed to this skepticism and has accordingly also been governing practice. All Swedish studies made on institutional groups indicate that institutional life (as quoted from one of the recent studies) "reinforces alienation, apathy and negative self-image, as well as making identification with a criminal way of life easier, not harder, to accept."

Whereas the social welfare boards are reluctant to use, on the one hand, the noninstitutional measures of admonition and warning, directives as to living conditions and supervision, and, on the other hand, the measure of sending a young person to a juvenile welfare school, there is a marked positive approach to various noncompulsory-noncoercive measures such as aid, advice, and support, and, in the case where the young person must be taken care of, placement in a private home (foster home). Statistics show that in 1973[5] there were 11,301 young persons over fifteen years of age placed in private homes. In the same year, there were 590 young persons over fifteen years of age in the juvenile welfare schools and an additional 747 minors on probational leave and parole.

DUE PROCESS OF LAW AND CRIME PREVENTION

The twentieth century in most countries has seen a variety and multitude of new procedural and treatment methods and facilities developed especially for the young offender. More and more categories of juvenile offenders have been removed from the traditional scope of criminal justice to be adjudicated and disposed of by established sociojudicial authorities such as juvenile and family courts, or by socioadministrative agencies such as the Scandinavian social (juvenile) welfare boards.[6] The very often recurrent question is how this continuous reform corresponds to *the fundamental principle of justice* in that a measure should be used only when it is legally authorized and in a manner which is likely to promote legal security as well as public and individual crime prevention.[7]

---

5. As for the situation on December 31.
6. Denmark and Norway have child welfare board systems very similar to the Swedish system. The first child welfare act was adopted in Norway (1895).
7. See *Juvenile Justice*, (1 Uppsala: Almquist and Wilksells, 1960. pp. 138 et seq.

The social welfare board system focuses its attention upon the individual need of the offender in order to prevent further crime on his behalf. Formal procedures, consideration of public law obedience, and the use of compulsory/coercive measures seem to contradict and complicate the application of the principle of individualized social welfare. However, a contradiction does not necessarily exist between the demand for legal security and the need for appropriate treatment, since legal security may be strongly called for out of consideration for primarily psychological and pedagogical aspects of the treatment process. But the dilemma is still there.

With regard to the Swedish system, the development, the arrangements as to due process of law, and the present state of opinion may be summarized as follows:

The original Child Welfare Act of 1902 covered offenders only under the age of fifteen. The revised act of 1924 extended the jurisdiction of the child welfare board to those under eighteen. A further extention was made in 1934 and 1944 enabling the boards to deal also with offenders between eighteen and twenty-one providing the social situation required it. The public prosecutors were not empowered to waive prosecution in the case of a fifteen-to-eighteen-year-old offender in favor of measures to be taken by the boards until 1944. Before that year prosecution was waived in an informal way. The age of eighteen is still the upper age limit for this type of waivers.

The development depicted has brought about an increasing stream of young offenders to the social welfare boards, including those who have committed serious crimes and have considerable criminal records. This, in turn, has raised the public demand for more strict procedures, not least in the cases of deprivation of liberty. According to its underlying philosophy the boards used to work very informally in the classical administrative way. Not until the revised Child Welfare Act of 1960 was a strong move made toward rules for a more pronounced legality and stronger legal safeguards in the form of representation by counsel and so forth. Gradually a special submission and appellate system has developed. Thus, in a matter of deprivation of liberty the case could always be surrendered to a *special administrative tribunal* at the county level, set up for social welfare matters in dispute. This should always be done in cases of a young person over fifteen years of age, when his parents do not agree to the decision of the social welfare board. The county tribunal is composed of a chairman, who shall be learned in law and have judicial experience, and four or at least three other members who are laymen elected by the county government. However informal the hearings in the tribunal may be, the procedures in most essential respects meet the needs for due process of law. In addition there are appellate courts, and capping the system is a Supreme Court in Administrative Matters. It should be added that the *ombudsman* exercises control of the system (by means of, among other things, inspections).

From a mere formal point of view, then, it can be properly said that the present social welfare board system offers sufficient legal safeguards. But evidently this fact has come to affect the work of the boards in a way, it is argued, which can risk the goodwill of the system and the good relations needed between the boards and the young persons and their parents whom they are to deal with. Therefore there are strong suggestions in the direction of surrendering all cases of administrative deprivation of liberty to the county tribunal, hereby strengthening legal security and at the same time facilitating the social welfare boards to work in an informal, open, and noncompulsory atmosphere—in order to establish better contacts with the young persons and their parents and in order on the whole to gain goodwill and public understanding. This arrangement could be regarded as a significant step along the lines generally advocated in the international discussion about *diversion* and—as to procedures—will no doubt promote a development in accordance with the opinion held, for example, by the U.S. Supreme Court in *Re Gault* (387, U.S. 1, 1967).

A government drafting committee is about to make recommendations in the direction mentioned. The committee is also considering a stricter jurisdiction of the social welfare boards as to young offenders and some reforms in the area of measures available to the boards.

CHANGE OF JURISDICTION AND MEASURES

The age of criminal responsibility and the age of civil majority are limits which most likely have an important bearing upon the jurisdiction of special juvenile adjudicating and disposing authorities. The early recognition in Scandinavia of comparatively high age limits for criminal responsibility most certainly explains the question why no juvenile courts were established in Scandinavia. Of course, it seems strange that the juvenile court and the child welfare board systems arose completely independent of each other. The first child welfare board act was adopted in Norway in 1895, and the first juvenile court act originated from Illinois in 1899. There were no references made by the respective lawmakers to any other system. It was evidently not known of. As a matter of fact, however, Norway set the minimum age of criminal responsibility at fourteen in 1896 and Sweden and Denmark set that age at fifteen in 1902 and 1905, respectively. It seems as if these high age limits automatically cut off all discussions as to a juvenile court alternative with jurisdiction also over juveniles "under age."

In the same way, the age of civil majority has influenced the choice of upper age limit for the competence of the social welfare boards. The maximum age of twenty-one was set when the age of civil majority was twenty-one. When that age was lowered to twenty in 1969, the upper age in the Child Welfare Act was changed accordingly to twenty. The same process was to be expected when the age of civil majority was further lowered to eighteen in 1974. By that time, however, the task was given to the drafting committee, mentioned above, to consider the consequences on the Child Welfare Act. Even if there is some support for the idea of keeping those offenders between eighteen and twenty years of age who are in special need for social care and protection within the scope of the social welfare system, it does not seem quite appropriate, it is argued, to retain a *"parens patriae* jurisdiction."* over persons who have attained civil majority. The committee will probably propose the maximum age limit at eighteen. If so, special arrangements have to be made for coordinating correctional and social welfare services to the benefit of those young adults who are in need of such aid and assistance generally provided by the social welfare system.

As to the measures the committee is considering some very radical changes. Statistics show, as indicated above, that compulsory preventive measures such as admonitions and warnings, directives of a young person's living conditions, and supervision are being less frequently used by the social welfare boards. The boards instead increasingly work with measures such as aid, advice, and support on a voluntary, noncoercive basis. There is a growing conviction that unless the young person and his parents are willing to accept the help of the board, such help will be of no value. In the same way traditional supervision will preferably be substituted for a noncompulsory system of *contact persons* in respect of the young offenders.[8] The aim is to involve constructively the young person in his own rehabilitation. If he does not want to be helped, as suggested, he has only to say so. This does not mean, of course, a total freedom from restrictions and coercive measures. But they should be limited to a minimum use. Present practice in the field and the underlying philosophy will probably influence the drafting committee to propose the abolition of the system of admonition and warning and directives concerning a young person's living conditions, upon which he

_____

8.   This system has been in use for some time.

has not agreed. Similarly, present rules on compulsory supervision will most likely be deleted.

In the light of international practice the discussed changes may seem strange. It will be remembered, as an example, the extensive use in England of police cautioning. However, the negative experience of compulsory measures within the Swedish social welfare system cannot be overlooked. And the entire field of treatment policies certainly is wide open to undoctrinary thinking and continually new endeavors.

Along the same line is the Swedish consideration of radically limiting public care in an institution to a period not exceeding, as a general rule, three months. Long institutional periods very often give unsatisfactory results. Therefore, placing a young person in an institution, where needed, it is argued, should be only the initial step and link in "a chain of treatment" primarily composed by noncompulsory follow-up measures.

SCREENING AND DIVERSION

The Swedish system of juvenile justice may be generally characterized by the watchwords—on the one hand, coordination, cooperation, amalgamation; and, on the other hand, procedural and treatmental diversion. In this system, as in any combined system of administrative and judicial juvenile agencies, the great dilemma is the question of selection with regard to those persons who are over the age of criminal responsibility. By tradition the systems vary considerably. In the English system the power of discretion to prosecute in the case of a young offender is vested in the police. In the Swedish system the public prosecutor holds a key position. Even if it might be said that his role as to the fifteen-to-eighteen-year-old offenders has become merely a routine to waive prosecution, he still has the final decision. To lay this responsibility on the social welfare board would in a sense seem logical but might on the other hand become seriously detrimental to the efforts of restricting the measures of the social welfare system to those on a voluntary and noncompulsory basis. In practice, the prosecutors and the boards work in close cooperation to the benefit of the young person. Evidently the prosecutor sometimes has to compromise from the strict standpoint of his natural role, thus leaving the boards with the ideological burden of handling also very serious cases in which compulsory measures hardly can be avoided. This is not to say that the interest of diversion necessarily could be better promoted by establishing an independent screening authority. However, such an agency, as recently proposed to be integrated in the Canadian system of juvenile justice,[9] might be a useful instrument in the application of a policy which considers individual as well as general crime prevention in the field. As the discussion intensifies on differentiation and diversion, a more definite stand has to be taken also to the question of screening. So far this matter has not been more closely examined in Sweden. But the changes of jurisdiction and measures under consideration will certainly demand that special attention be paid to the subject.

9. *Young Persons in Conflict with the Law*, A Report of the Solicitor General's Committee on Proposals for new legislation to replace the Juvenile Delinquent Act (Ottawa, 1975).

9

Tradition and Innovation in Child Care in Nigeria

Tolani Asuni

It is necessary to distinguish between what is happening in Nigeria and what I believe should be happening. If one considers the title of an old book, *The Juvenile in Delinquent Society*, one will tend to see the juvenile delinquent as one reacting to a society in which some patterns of behavior are not consistent with the morals put forward by the same society. In fact, they are often contradictory. Since we cannot readily correct this contradiction and hypocrisy in society, much as it is desirable, we have to turn our attention to the area where our intervention can be pragmatic and effective.

If one sees the delinquent child as one reacting to some unpleasant, threatening, or painful situation which is usually in the family or in the school, one might be able to do something about it. What can be done should not be an imitation of what happens elsewhere.

My impression is that we are not making enough use of traditional methods of dealing with the problem of juvenile delinquency. While some families in overdeveloped countries do not seem to have much control over their children anymore, in societies like mine families still do have appreciable control, and this control can be utilized in the prevention and handling of the problems of children. I believe that in our developmental programs, we have to bear this in mind.

If we take, for example, the introduction of universal primary education in Nigeria, one can see dangers ahead. What is being advocated is that education will be free for all children. This sounds laudable, but what are the implications of this? One important implication is that the participation and concern of parents in the education of their children, instead of being enhanced, will be minimized. At the extreme, some parents will abrogate their responsibility entirely. The efforts and contribution of parents toward the education of their children win for the parents the love and respect of the children. It is from this love and respect that proper control of the children derives. The state or government is an intangible, anonymous factor to which love and respect cannot be transferred. My view is that education should be made available to all and that parents should make some contribution to enable their children to take advantage of the educational facilities provided. It is not enough to argue that the parents pay taxes. The taxes are used for many other items in society, and the children should not be expected to identify their education as one of the items. Perhaps, when the society is sophisticated enough, education may be free. Even then, I have my doubts.

Let us now look into the system for dealing with juvenile delinquents. There is some strong evidence that the problem is on the increase, but the modern facilities available for dealing with it are not increasing proportionately, and the traditional system of dealing with it is becoming inappropriate, especially in the urban centers.

The juvenile delinquent is the young person who runs afoul of the law and is caught. Therefore, the bulk of the juvenile delinquents have been caught by the police, and the commonest offense is stealing. There is another group who are reported by their parents or guardians as being beyond control. There is a third group who are picked up by welfare officers who periodically raid public places like markets at night with the specific purpose of picking up these youngsters.

They are all presented in a juvenile court, usually presided over by a trained magistrate and consisting of laymen and laywomen. Prior to the presentation in the court, the welfare officers have collected as much information as possible within the competence and mobile power. These children are kept in remand homes while their cases and background are being investigated. The remand home with which I am most familiar is situated about a mile from the periphery of the town. It has no telephone, and no transportation is available. The staff in the remand home vary in quality. Some of them teach children. There is no psychologist on the staff. Occasionally, a child with an obvious psychiatric disturbance is referred to the psychiatric hospital. There is no child guidance clinic to which the obviously disturbed children can be sent. There is no medical doctor in attendance, but one of the staff members functions as a nurse. The authorities are aware of these deficiencies, but the financial and manpower resources available are not sufficient to improve the situation. The question may well be asked: Why embark on such a system of remand if it cannot be done properly? The frequent response is that we have to start somewhere.

The two most important methods of disposal are probation and committal to an approved school. As in many other places, and perhaps more so in developing countries, the case loads of probation officers are overwhelming. The few probation officers have other duties to perform as well.

Children who have been committed to approved schools for training have better chances than other underprivileged children who have not violated the law. And it has been known that some parents have gone to report some minor misdemeanor of their children to the authorities, asking the authorities to admit the children to approved schools, not because the children are not manageable, nor because they have committed a serious offense, or that they cannot be treated in any other noninstitutional manner, but because the parents are anxious to give these children the opportunity of vocational training which they would not have otherwise.

One wonders whether this system is not out of step in the context of developing countries, where the social, medical, and educational facilities are still very inadequate for the general population. On the other hand, it may be argued that since these are children in trouble and if not treated properly, may be the criminals of tomorrow, the special provisions made for them are justifiable. It may be a fact of "a stitch in time saves nine".

A proposal has been made to involve the community in the probation process, not only because of the shortage of probation officers, but also because of the principle of the poor self-image of the juvenile offenders, which may be improved by giving them the opportunity of identifying with respectable members of the community. It was proposed:

1. To compile a register of respectable adult members of the community—priests, business people, teachers, etc.
2. To visit or write to them asking if they are interested and willing to participate in a community project to help delinquent children.
3. To invite and screen those interested and willing to participate in an orientation course to help them in the project. It will be pointed out that the course will be useful to them not only for the project, but also in their own understanding and upbringing of their children.
4. The children on probation will need to be classified to find out in which households of the adults they may fit best in terms of age, sex, type of offense, and type of family background. The children will then be allocated accordingly, also taking the preference of the adult into consideration.
5. These cases will then be reviewed at regular intervals, and the lay adults should have ready and easy access to the professional probation officers to bring up

crises which may develop. The professional support
of the project should be readily available.

It is envisaged that it will boost the positive self-image of the
delinquent child to say among his friends from time to time that
he is going to visit the respectable adult whom the others cannot
visit. It will also boost his positive self-image to be favorably
acknowledged and spoken to in public by this respectable
adult. Since the status of such an adult in the community will be
higher than that of the professional probation officer, and since
the relationship between the adult and the child will be informal
and devoid of red tape and bureaucracy as much as possible, it is
envisaged that the child will identify more readily with him than
with the professional probation officer, and consequently the
probation will be more successful.

This is an interesting and worthwile proposal which may have
other advantages in addition to easing the heavy case loads of
the professional probation officers. One possible advantage may
be the increased tolerance and understanding of delinquent
behavior by the community. It will be relatively inexpensive,
and if it cannot do as much good as envisaged it will not do any
harm either. The same idea, modified, of course, can be used in
some cases sent to approved schools. This will not be a novel
idea, as it has been a long-established practice for some difficult
children to be boarded by their family with a loving, kindly, but
firm adult, known to the family. Sometimes this adult is a
member of the extended family of the child.

This proposal is based on the traditional love of children in
the community which is characterized, for example, by barren
adults unofficially adopting children of relatives. It is regarded
to be unfortunate when an adult, especially a married adult, has
no children of his own. The status of a family is enhanced by the
number of children they have. The situation may change with
the propaganda on the planned family, but while it is still as it is

it can be used to the advantage of delinquent children. At least it is worth trying.

Even though this proposal was put forward as a pilot project several years ago, it has not been implemented. It may be that there is some reluctance to innovate. On the other hand, it is a fact that those concerned are so overwhelmed with other assignments that they have not even been able to compile the initial register. There is also the movement of staff from one station to another, and this is a project which needs the continued stay of staff in the same station to be effectively implemented. Now that the country has been split into smaller states, it may be easier to implement the proposal.

At the moment it is mainly the children of the underprivileged that are consumers of the services for delinquent children. It will be too simple and erroneous to infer from this that the children of the privileged do not get involved in delinquent behavior. The delinquency of the children of the elite is often contained in their environment, and they are protected from getting into the system. There is some indication that proportionally more children of the elite get involved in the illicit use of drugs, but they are seldom arrested for it.

I believe that developing countries are in the unique position of not being overburdened by long-practiced systems which are difficult to change, and therefore are able to innovate their own system congruent with their social and traditional conditions. The fact that the financial and manpower resources available are inadequate to copy the pattern in developed countries should not be regarded as a disadvantage but rather as a challenge to use other social and cultural resources available.

It is a pity that not enough research is being done in developing countries in the area of juvenile delinquency, and consequently, the tendency is to accept the findings of research done in developed countries as applicable in developing countries.

The evaluation of the system practiced is hardly talked about, let alone put into effect. Research and pilot studies done in developing countries, and done transculturally, may well add more to the body of knowledge of the problem and throw some light on how to deal with it better.

10

The Faces of Juvenile Justice in Canada

V. Lorne Stewart

AN EVOLVING PLAN FOR JUVENILE JUSTICE

To trace the metamorphosis of the Canadian juvenile court and the justice practices and services that surround it may be of value to countries endeavoring to establish their own juvenile justice systems. This melding of the basic tenets of juvenile court philosophy and the insights of those disciplines and agencies that have paid special heed to children has been a task no easier to accomplish in Canada than elsewhere. The attempt to strike a balance between the needs and rights of children and of society and to ply Horace's "via media" in cases where misconduct has been spawned in conditions far beyond the child's control or understanding is no simple juridical exercise. In this regard, Canada has its own peculiar problem constitutional in nature, which has had a salutory effect upon the development of a unified system.

A second obstacle blocking the creation of a homogeneous application of law and practice has been the geographical nature of the country with its international border stretching for over 5,000 miles between itself and the United States. How can a system "equal to all and above all equally" be structured in a land mass that extends "from the Beaufort Sea to the Alaska

Panhandle, from the Strait of Juan de Fuca to Passamaquoddy Bay,"[1] and clear across the northern shore of the North American continent to the Atlantic Ocean? Yet the philosophy built into its Juvenile Delinquents Act guaranteeing rights, protection, and help does apply in this vast space. Of course, in the larger urban centers more is offered with well-established juvenile courts, frequently surrounded by ancillary clinical and social services of contemporary design. First, let us consider the legal reasons for the direction taken in Canada. The division of powers between the federal and provincial governments has posed substantial difficulties in arriving at a working solution to the problem of children who contravene the law. The British North America Act,[2] Canada's constitutional document, empowers the central government to control persons within the nation in criminal matters. Thus, crime is made the exclusive responsibility of the federal parliament. The provinces, however, are given responsibility to establish the judicial machinery needed to administer the law and to regulate the civil status of persons.

Later, as we deal with Canada's special law designed to deal with the legal transgressions of children, the Juvenile Delinquents Act, we will see how this division of powers has encumbered attempts to treat delinquency as a social condition. In other words, we will see why Canada's juvenile courts are essentially criminal courts calibrated to the age of its clients and carrying with them the ingredients of a "fair" hearing through recognized and practiced procedures of due process but, at the same time, bearing the burden and disadvantages attached to a criminal-court type of procedure. For the present we will follow

---

1. National Film Board of Canada, *Between Friends/Entre Amis,* Ottawa, McClelland and Stewart, 1976.
2. The British North America Act (London; 1867, 30-31 Vict.).

the growth of the criminal law in Canada to see how it has applied to children.

Historically the system has sprung from British tradition and experience, and nowhere is this more apparent than in the area of criminal justice. British precedent, philosophy, and procedures have formed its warp and woof. This experience in judicial decision-making was limited for years by dependence upon the legal decisions of the English courts. However, in 1867 Canada moved from colonial to dominion status, and a new day dawned with the formation of one national, central government presiding over a federation of provinces. It took some years for this government to create a code of behavior of its own to apply equally throughout the country and with diminishing dependence upon British decisions.

One of the earliest references to the special treatment of young offenders in pre-Confederation Canada is found in An Act for the More Speedy Trial and Punishment of Juvenile Offenders (1857).

Whereas in order in certain cases to ensure the more speedy trial of juvenile offenders, and to avoid the evils of their long imprisonment previously to trial, it is expedient to allow of such offenders being proceeded against in a more summary manner than is now by law provided, and to give further power to bail them: Therefore, Her Majesty, by and with advice and consent of the Legislative Council and Assembly of Canada enacts as follows: . . .[3]

The act then set out such provisions as the following indicating a

---

3. An Act for the More Speedy Trial and Punishment of Juvenile Offenders (Ottawa, 1957, 20 Vict.), p. 103.

growing awareness of the special needs of the young and allowing the use of judicial discretion on their behalf but at the same time guarding the rights of the community:

> Persons of not more than sixteen years of age committing certain offences, may be summarily convicted by two Justices.

> Justices may dismiss the accused if they deem it expedient not to inflict any punishment.

> Case may be sent for trial in the usual manner if the Justices think fit.[4]

In 1892, An Act Respecting the Criminal Law was introduced and passed in the Canadian Parliament. It has such things as the following to say about young offenders, particularly with respect to their culpability and responsibility before the law:

Children under seven.
No person shall be convicted of an offence by reason of any act or omission of such person when under the age of seven years.

Children between seven and fourteen.
No person shall be convicted of an offence by reason of an act or omission of such person when of the age of seven, but under the age of fourteen years, unless he was competent to know the nature and consequences of his conduct, and to appreciate that it was wrong.[5]

---

4. Ibid., pp. 103-105.
5. Crankshaw, James, *The Criminal Code of Canada,* Montreal, 1894, Whiteford and Theoret.

In a section entitled Trial of Juvenile Offenders for Indictable Offences, the Code set down the procedure to be followed in serious cases. However, even a casual examination of its provision shows how little it attempted innovations to meet the special needs of the very young. Using the same classical terminology, methods, and dispositions, it stated that in the case of a person charged with theft, when his age did not exceed sixteen years, he should:

upon conviction thereof in *open court* upon his own confession or upon proof, before any two or more justices, be committed to the *common gaol* or other place of confinement within the jurisdiction of such justices, then to be imprisoned, with or without *hard labour,* for any term not exceeding *three months,* or in the discretion of such justices, shall forfeit and pay such, not exceeding *twenty dollars*, as such justices adjudge.[6]

The italics are the author's. It is intended to show that juveniles were still being arraigned as adults; were appearing in open court; were being sentenced with or without hard labor to institutions housing adults and designed for the more sophisticated. However, at the point of judicial decision, it was possible to temper severity with mercy and to impose sanctions in the form of fines and moderated sentences.

In 1893 the first Canadian law dealing exclusively with children in need of care, protection, and control was passed. It was entitled An Act for the Prevention of Cruelty to, and Better Protection of Children.[7] In it was a blueprint for the establish-

6. Ibid., p. 693.
7. An Act for the Prevention of Cruelty to, and Better Protection of Children, Revised Statutes of Ontario, (Toronto, 1894, 56 Vict.).

ment of Children's Aid Societies and for the commitment to them of neglected children by court order. As in Britain, there continued "The conflict between the judicial and criminal welfare functions of the courts."[8] The application of the statute to the problem of delinquency was limited by the jurisdictional division described earlier. An attempt was made to remedy this defect with the passage of another law, entitled "An Act Respecting the Arrest, Trial and Imprisonment of Youthful Offenders,[9] passed in 1894. In it provision was made for private trials for offenders under sixteen years of age; and for their incarceration, prior to sentence, separately from adults.

THE JUVENILE DELINQUENTS ACT (1908)

Canada's first nationwide legislation to deal solely with juvenile delinquency became law in 1908.[10] It remained on the statute books, undisturbed for twenty years. However, on October 24, 1928, a conference was called by the minister of justice to review the situation and to make recommendations with respect to legislative changes. The fifty persons who attended included provincial attorneys-general, legislative law officers, juvenile court judges, probation officers, and other interested persons. The outcome was a rewritten act which became law in 1929.[11] This act has continued in force to the present with very

---

8. Barbara Wootton, "The Juvenile Court," *The Criminal Law Review,* London, Sweet and Maxwell Press, 1961, p. 671.
9. An Act Respecting the Arrest, Trial and Imprisonment of Youthful Offenders (Ottawa, 1894, 57-58 Vict.).
10. The Juvenile Delinquents Act, Revised Statutes of Canada (Ottawa, 1908).
11. The Juvenile Delinquents Act, Revised Statutes of Canada (Ottawa, 1929).

few amendments. However, in recent years it has become the subject of increasing criticism.

The Juvenile Delinquents Act is legislation in the language and spirit of the first half of this century—the so-called century of the child. It did not spring into existence overnight. It was but a national expression of the rise of a special kind of justice designed for children in a number of widely dispersed areas in the world. The emphasis was upon prevention and protection, and it was felt that the only way to deal with crime was to improve the environment surrounding children. This interest and spirit of the 1908 legislation is well summarized in his following words:

> The rights of parents are sacred and ought not to be lightly interfered with, but they may be forfeited by abuse. Paramount to the rights of parents is the right of every child to a fair chance of growing up to be an honest, respectable citizen. What chance has the daughter of a prostitute, if left with her mother, to be other than a prostitute, or the son of a thief to be other than a thief? And why should this girl be condemned, through no fault of her own, to a life of prostitution, or that boy, unwittingly, to a career of crime? The State, too, has rights and ought not to stand idly by while children are trained, either by evil example or by neglect, to disobey her laws.[12]

Out of this type of social concern for children sprang the Canadian juvenile court. Its philosophical base and objectives were well delineated in the following section:

---

12. W. L. Scott, Q.C., *The Juvenile Court in Law and the Juvenile Court in Action,* Ottawa, Canadian Welfare Council, 1927; and in John E. Crankshaw, *Criminal Code of Canada,* Toronto, Carswell, 6th ed., 1935, p. 1531.

This Act shall be liberally construed to the end that its purpose may be carried out, namely, that the care and custody and discipline of a juvenile delinquent shall approximate as nearly as may be that which should be given by its parents, and that as far as practicable every juvenile delinquent shall be treated, not as a criminal, but as a misdirected and misguided child, and one needing aid, encouragement, help and assistance.[13]

The court itself was designed carefully as a flexible and active instrument for social control. Judges were to be selected for their sincere interest and knowledge of children and their families. Children themselves were seen, not as diminutive criminals, but as ordinary youngsters needing special care and direction once they became delinquent. A deliberate intent was exercised to avoid giving them a bad name. The term "juvenile delinquent" was accepted in an attempt to find a replacement for the harsh adult term for criminal activity. The young delinquent was seen as the boy next door who like most adults at some point in their lives makes mistakes in judgment. The home was still to be regarded as society's strongest social force, but because parents are human beings and too often default in their obligations they need help in raising their young. To leave a child in his own home under the added care of a probation officer was deemed to be infinitely better than sending him to an institution. Intrusion into the privacy of the home was to be exercised only as a last resort.

From the beginning the definition of juvenile delinquency caused great concern: a government trying to think its way around adult criminal semantics and associated stigmatization found trouble in describing the types of juvenile misbehavior that required coercive action. Where the intent was to

---

13. The Juvenile Delinquent Act, op. cit., p. 3523, s. 38

decriminalize and to treat in a new rehabilitative way the harshness of Code-defined offenses seemed out of place. Then, too, children engage in noncriminal acts frequently deemed much more serious and embarrassing in the eyes of their elders than specific forms of illegal conduct. How should the incorrigible, the unmanageable, the truant, the sex offender, the glue sniffer, the runaway be dealt with? And what name should be attached to theft, arson, rape, assault, and so on if they are not called crimes? The term "juvenile delinquency" invented elsewhere to describe an ever increasing heterogeneous galaxy of problems was built into the Canadian legislation. The trouble, of course, was that judicial discretion was sorely taxed when judges sought help from the behavioral sciences. Seeking advice concerning a host of complex social-legal problems, their judgments often were regarded as discretionary, unfair, and unjust by children, parents, and professionals. Judges who had done their best to keep a reasonable balance between the needs and rights of youngsters appearing before them found themselves in the middle of a battle about priorities. It cannot be denied that the growth of the Civil Rights movement in the United States has been instrumental in changing the direction of the juvenile court in North America. The case of Gerald Gault has had its effect upon Canadian thinking in the field of juvenile justice. The Juvenile Delinquents Act with its allowance for a wide use of discretion, flexibility, and wide jurisdiction in noncriminal matters, having served its purpose when hopes were high but services sparse in having to give way to a new order of practice and procedures. In a sense, we have witnessed the rise and fall of the juvenile court.

A CHILDREN AND YOUNG PERSONS ACT
PROPOSED (1965)

Various attempts have been made to persuade the federal government to rewrite the Juvenile Delinquents Act or to provide a successor of more contemporary design. In 1961 a special committee of the Department of Justice was appointed with a mandate to:

(a) inquire into and report upon the nature and extent of the problem of juvenile delinquency in Canada;

(b) hold discussions with appropriate representatives of provincial governments with the object of finding ways and means of ensuring effective cooperation between federal and provincial governments acting within their respective constitutional jurisdiction; and

(c) make recommendations concerning steps that might be taken by the Parliament and Government of Canada to meet the problem of juvenile delinquency in Canada.[14]

This committee traveled throughout Canada and met with persons engaged in work with delinquent children. Its report was released in 1965 and consisted of one hundred recommendations proposing radical changes in the juvenile justice system. Included were recommendations that a greater effort should be made to extend the juvenile court concept and its benefits throughout the country; to call conferences; to provide government leadership aimed at equalizing and standardizing services; the abandonment of the term "juvenile delinquent" and the adoption of the designations of "child offender" and "young offender"; raising the age of criminal responsibility from seven years to either ten or twelve years; changing the title of the

---

14. "Juvenile Delinquency in Canada," Report of the Department of Justice, Ottawa, Queen's Printer, 1965.

statute from "the Juvenile Delinquents Act to the Children and Young Persons Act; removing status offenses from the federal jurisdiction; limiting the length of committal to training school; setting firm controls over the taking of statements from juveniles; allowing the press to attend court sessions by right except where expressly prohibited by the judge; providing legal representation similar in nature to the "law-guardian" system.

While the report of the committee reflected growing disenchantment with the Juvenile Delinquents Act, it failed to take shape as a bill before the House of Commons. Residual sentiment still favored the Juvenile Delinquents Act and its friendly paternal approach to the problems of children. In any event, the winds of political change were blowing and the committee's report became moribund. Years were to pass before another serious attempt was made to bring juvenile law in line with contemporary thought about child guidance and control and individual rights.

THE SWING OF THE PENDULUM TOWARD DIVERSION

Meanwhile questions were being asked in many places about the effectiveness of the juvenile court. The unrealistic expectancy that this legal innovation invented in Chicago in 1899 could be adopted easily in other cultural settings, and could in fact rid every country of its delinquency problems in short order was a fatal assumption and hope. In Canada as elsewhere, the juvenile court became a dumping ground for the child-raising problems of parents, schools, and social agencies. Decision by authority became a fashion, and judges were forced into impossible positions to attempt to do by authority what others were unable to do by noncoercive casework and by other fashionable methods. Too frequently the courts were forced to exercise jurisdiction in areas where social default had already eroded constructive effort.

Strange is the fact that with the clamor to abolish the kindly

Juvenile Delinquents Act the pendulum has swung once again in the direction of community-based responsibility and action. Why has this happened? One answer is that the juvenile court, having failed to perform the miracles assigned to it, has lost much of its glamor. Another is that we have at last come face to face with the fact that too many children have been processed needlessly through the justice system. Furthermore, we are no longer as confident that the fatherly or motherly judge can reach through to every child irrespective of the cultural, psychological, and other differences that separate them.

Then, too, the theorists have stirred the waters of confidence by raising questions about stigma and self-fulfilling prophecies and the possibility that the journey to court may be a damaging and traumatic experience for an ingenuous youngster. There are those of course who believe that a sensitive and perceptive judge can so order his proceedings that to appear there may have a therapeutic effect on the child.[15]

Much has been learned about children since the juvenile court came into being. It seems appropriate, despite negative opinions about the "medical model," that we should now call upon the educational, behavioral, and social sciences who have been developing diagnostic and treatment techniques for many years to move in to accomplish what has been asked unfairly of the juvenile court judges, usually untrained in this type of knowledge and practice. The latent and available resources in the community are being challenged anew to search for answers so difficult to find in a "decision-by-authority" atmosphere, especially in cases where it is felt that the courts should not intrude.

In 1961 a former English Magistrate and social scientist com-

---

15. David Reifen, "Therapeutic Use of the Court Setting," *The Juvenile Court in a Changing Society,* Philadelphia, Univ. of Pennsylvania Press, 1972.

pared the community services with those available fifty years earlier:

> Things are dramatically different now. Today the variety of facilities available outside the judicial machine for dealing with the problem child or child with a problem is positively dazzling. In face of this luxuriance, it is hard indeed to believe that it can be necessary to bring such children before the courts.[16]

That prophetic statement might well be applied to the Canadian situation today.

YOUNG PERSONS IN CONFLICT WITH THE LAW (1975)

Canada has continued to rethink this matter of young people who break the law and to take inventory of its social potential to solve problems of children without the overuse of the justice system. After two years of intensive study of the issues and responding to widespread public and professional opinion, a committee appointed by the Solicitor General of Canada produced a document entitled "Young Persons in Conflict with the Law."[17] It included a model draft act and a commentary prepared for wide distribution and aimed at federal legislation. It was a radical departure from the Juvenile Delinquents Act and was felt to reflect a changing mood with respect to young people. It envisaged a more important role for the new youth court in areas of graver concern pertaining to older youngsters. But it took a strong position that better ways must be found to deal with the more ingenuous young. The following major changes in the law were recommended:

---

16. Barbara Wootton, "The Juvenile Court," op. cit., pp. 66.
17. "Young Persons in Conflict with the Law," Report of the Solicitor General of Canada (Ottawa; 1975).

1. The Juvenile Delinquents Act should be abolished.

2. The omnibus offence of "juvenile delinquent" should be succeeded by greater specificity in charging.

3. The age of criminal responsibility should be raised from seven to fourteen years.

4. Eighteen years should be set as the upper jurisdictional limit for initiating new action.

5. The youth court should have exclusive jurisdiction to deal with young persons between the ages of fourteen and eighteen years.

6. A formal mechanism should be established to provide pre-court screening to facilitate the diversion of young persons from the court process.

7. The right to legal counsel or the assistance of some "responsible person" should be guaranteed.

8. Limits should be set upon the length of supervisory or placement orders thus reversing the current practice of open-ended, indefinite sanctions.

9. Pre-disposition reports should be mandatory in cases where probation or custody are being considered.

10. Provision should be made for a systematic judicial review of cases.

11. An administrative review agency should be established with responsibility to monitor the quality of service at specified times with respect to every young person on probation or in open or secure custody.

Following publication of the report a further thorough canvassing of public opinion took place for two years. This has resulted in revised proposals issued by the solicitor general.[18] While agreeing with most of the committee's report, it suggested

---

18. "Highlights of Proposed Legislation for Young Offenders," Solicitor General of Canada (Ottawa, 1977).

the following changes:

(1) that the title be "The Young Offenders Act"; (2) that the recommended minimum age of criminal responsibility be twelve rather than fourteen, (3) that the upper age of jurisdiction for the youth court be set at eighteen for the whole country (provincial variations are to be allowed for the time being ranging from sixteen to eighteen years), (4) that the proposed nonjudicial "screening agency" be abandoned but the principle of screening and diversion be retained, (5) that the youth court should be relieved of responsibility for dealing with less serious offences, and that ". . .the application of the formal court process should be limited to those instances when a young person cannot be adequately dealt with by other social or legal means."[19]

Whatever the ultimate decision by the Parliament of Canada, a new tone in the prevention of delinquency and the treatment of the young offender seems imminent.

CONCLUSION

While the faces of juvenile justice differ there are fundamental similarities throughout Canada. The home is still regarded as the most important socializing force in the rearing of the young. To this end the continuation of strong support for parents to enable them to fulfill their obligations is assured by social policy. The diversion fashion is becoming consolidated in community action, and cases that previously found their way into court are being dealt with by other means. Communities are responding to the challenge by innovation and by stronger support of traditional services. Children are being removed from their homes only as a last resort, and then under strict regulation and control. Training schools are being replaced by smaller units in many places, and even these are being bypassed where it is deemed wiser to use group homes. The movement is in the direc-

---

19. Ibid., p. 6.

tion of an organizational structure and service-delivery system which allows the young person to remain in his or her own home or general home area wherever possible. The pressure to avoid the contaminant features so frequently inevitable in an institutional environment is resulting in a new design of care and supervision. Common sense and experience have led Canada to proceed in this direction with consummate caution. There has been no wholesale closing of training schools, nor is there likely to be so long as the need exists for some form of secure care in the interests of both the young person and the community. It would seem that the juvenile court will become a youth court within a unified Family Court structure. The offenders will be older; the charges will be more serious; and the need for greater care and competence in judicial decision-making will become more necessary. The group of young persons between twelve and eighteen years—not yet adults but capable of committing acts of the most serious nature—will need to be tried by judges who know much more than the law. Even then, to be effective, judges will have to have readily available an extended spectrum of helping services despite the suggested swing toward the use of "coercive sanctions appropriate to the seriousness of the offence."[20]

The Canadian juvenile court, historically contained within parameters to official discretion and subject to basic principles of procedural due process, is entering a new metamorphic phase. It is becoming more seriously a court but within an enlarged family law jurisdiction. With the possibility that many of its former areas of responsibility may be vacated, the resulting vacuum will need to be filled quickly by other agencies of social control. Social policy can be seen today reaching back into the community endeavoring to revitalize traditional institutions in order to solve the problems of young people with determination and dignity.

---

20. Orman C. Ketcham "National Standards for Juvenile Justice," (Virginia Law Review vol. 63 no. 2 (1977).

Index

Abused children Adoption, 153
Alliance of NGO's, 4
Antilla, Inkeri, 49
Asuni, Tolani, 6, 151
Bruce, N., 6
Brantingham, Paul J., 45
Children and Young Persons Act, 5, 69, 165
Children in trouble, 69, 71
Children's hearing, 96
Community based facilities, 41
Correctional strategy, 53
Curran, J.H., 6
Canada, 147, 157-172
Chief public prosecutor, 136
Child Welfare Act, 139
Child Welfare Board, 141
Criminal responsibility, 73, 111, 115, 170
defense sociale, 111
Developing countries, 154
Diagnosis, 67
Disposition, 79, 83
Diversion, 43, 60, 109, 115, 118, 146, 167
England and Wales, 69-85
Faust, Frederick L., 45
Family Control, 151
Gault, Gerald, 2, 17, 20, 24, 143, 165

I.A.Y.M., 4
Individual rights, 36, 65
Institutions, 41
Intake, 63
Jones, Beti, 6, 87
Juvenile bureaus, 75, 77
Juvenile courts, 2, 9, 10, 11, 33, 43, 47, 78, 87, 88, 135
Juvenile Justice Act, 57
Jurisdiction, 33, 111, 138
Juvenile Delinquents Act, 158,162
Ketcham, Orm W., 4, 9-42
Kilbrandon report, 90,92
Laidlaw Foundation, 3
Lejins, P., 44
Luger, Milton, 4, 53
Mack, Julian, 12
Marshall, Peter, 5, 69
McGrath Foundation, 5
Murrey, George, 6, 87
McKeiver v. Pennsylvania, 19
N.C.C.D., 5
Neglected children, 35
New Scotland Yard, 5, 75
Norman, Sherwood, 50
Nigeria, 148, 151-156
Ombudsman, 65, 143
Panel, Children's, 98
Paulsen, Monrad, 2
Parens patriae, 9, 20, 145

173

Police cautions, 77
Police warnings, 93
Public policy, 57
Prevention, 43, 139
Petty Offence Judge, 112
Procurator, fiscal, 94
Private-public integration, 63
Qualified informant, 71
Reifen, David, 168
Reporter, 94
Russell Sage Foundation, 168
Scotland, 86-110
Scott, W.L., 163
Screening, 60, 146, 152, 171
Self-image, 152
Selih, Alenka, 6, 111
Sheriff court, 103
Social welfare boards, 135
Spencer, J., 6
Status offenders, 34, 46, 61, 63
Stewart, V. Lorne, 1, 157

Sweden, 135-150
Training schools, 41, 64, 171
Treatment, right to, 38, 40
United Nations Congress on the
    Prevention of Crime and the
    Treatment of Offenders:
    (Fifth.1975.Toronto-
    Geneva), 19, 32
    (Sixth.1980.Sydney), 3
U.N.S.D.R.I. (Rome), 3
United States of America, 9-68
Unified Family Court, 172
Volunteers, 35, 152
Ward, Frederick, 4, 43
Wootton, Barbara, 162, 169
Yugoslavia, 111-134
Youth Service Bureaus, 50
Young adult offender, 137
Young persons in conflict with
    the law, 147, 169
Young Offenders Act, 171